WHO KILLED STEPHEN WARD?

A DEATH IN 1963

By

Alex Duggan.

Copyright © Alex Duggan 2025

Table of Contents.

Part 1. I go from a corruptible to an incorruptible Crown.
Chapter 1. So much to live for. Why do some people kill themselves?
Chapter 2. Life before The Beatles.
Chapter 3. A dance to the music of time. Heading towards the sixties.
Chapter 4. She's in Parties. From swing music to swinging.

Part 2. They are fully satisfied with their own authority. 1961.
Chapter 5. We're not all going on a Summer Holiday. Cliveden.
Chapter 6. Casino Royal. The Secret Service club
Chapter 7. The banality of fame.
Chapter 8. Picture yourself on a boat on a river.
Chapter 9. Sex and drugs and Vodka Stolle.
Chapter 10. It was over twenty years ago today.

Part 3. Never make a defence or apology before you be accused.
Chapter 11. That was the year that was.
Chapter 12. The Winter of discontent.
Chapter 13. The mirror crack'd. Political reflections.
Chapter 14. Cunnilingus and psychiatry brought us to this. Things start getting sticky.
Chapter 15. The Old Bill and the Old Bailey.

Part 4. I see all the birds have flown away.
Chapter 16. The Goddess of the eternal court of history
Chapter 17. Christine in the box.
Chapter 18. Blondes have more fun.
Chapter 19. Miss Whiplash gives the police a good tongue lashing.
Chapter 20. Summing up and coming down.

Part 5. I have neither eyes to see, nor tongue to speak.
Chapter 21. Aftermath. Let it be Beatle-esque.
Chapter 22. Two thousand light years from home. Too much news in nineteen sixty-three.
Chapter 23. Infamy, infamy, they've all got it in for me.
Chapter 24. They think it's all over. It still isn't now.
Chapter 25. You can't always get what you want.

PART ONE

I go from a corruptible, to an

incorruptible Crown.

Chapter 1.

So much to live for.

This book started off as an investigation into the death of Dr Stephen Ward, the London osteopath mixed up in the Profumo Scandal in the early 1960's. The story goes that in July 1961 Ward introduced his friend Christine Keeler to the Secretary of State for War, John Profumo, who promptly went on to have an affair with her. At the same time Ward also introduced the nineteen-year-old Christine to the Russian Naval Attaché Yevgeny Ivanov, who also had sex with her. Christine and the two men soon separated and the whole thing seemed to have been forgotten. Over a year later Keeler had become involved with two other men, Lucky Gordon and Johnny Edgecombe. After Gordon was arrested for assaulting Christine, and Edgecombe had fired shots at her whilst she was at Ward's home in Wimpole Mews in December 1962, reporters quickly realised there was a bigger story behind the headlines. This one involved state secrets, a Russian, and nuclear warheads.

Questions continued to be asked in the early part of 1963, reaching the ears of people such as prime minister Harold Macmillan, the opposition leader Harold Wilson, and others such as the Home Secretary, the commander of the Metropolitan police, the heads of MI5 and MI6, plus certain members of the royal family. They knew Stephen Ward publicly as an established osteopath and a portrait artist of the rich and famous. Privately he had also been organising and attending what we would now call 'sex parties' which included some of the same rich and famous he had previously etched.

In March sixty-three there were concerns when Christine Keeler disappeared before giving evidence in the Edgecombe trial. It ended with Jack Profumo having to stand up in parliament and declare, "There was no impropriety whatsoever in my acquaintanceship with

Miss Keeler". He went on to say that Miss Keeler was a liar and was willing to sue anyone who questioned his integrity.

He had forgotten about a note he had left in which he called her *Darling*. When he realised there was evidence of the affair, he stood back up in Parliament a few weeks later and said that he was mistaken. In fact, he was the one who had lied, to his wife, to parliament, to the country, and himself. He then promptly resigned before any further questions could be asked. Christine disappeared again after lying in court during the Lucky Gordon trial.

A few months later it was Stephen Ward, the man with everything at the start of the sixties, who found himself in the dock of the highest court in England. He was facing a possible fourteen years in prison for living off the immoral earnings of prostitutes. He would take his own life before the jury reached a verdict, although there are now questions as to whether he died by his own hand, or another.

~

How does a man get to the point where he feels he has no other option but to kill himself? When does a life become so bad that the only good thing left is leaving it? There are around eighteen suicides every day in the United Kingdom, with three quarters of them being men. The reasons for this are many: Financial issues, addictions, relationship breakdowns, chronic pain, loneliness, mental health concerns, and the feeling of not being a man anymore. Quite often it will be the last person you expect who does it. By the age of fifty most people will know of someone who has committed suicide just as much as they know someone who has cancer.

This doesn't include those who sometimes think about taking their life, or those who get close and then change their mind. There are those who go through with the attempt, but for whatever reason (the process is not life threatening, or they are found and given help to recover) do not die. This group tends to have more women than men. It used to be said that these actions were 'a cry for help', as they quite often would call someone to say goodbye. Suicide has been with us for so long it is difficult to understand why we still haven't solved the problem.

One of the most well-known suicides is the story of Judas, a man so full of guilt about what his life had become that he hanged himself. The Bible connected suicide with sin the moment Judas put the noose around his neck. Going back further, the Greek philosopher Socrates was put on trial in 399 BC for corrupting the minds of the young. It was a made-up charge to try and stop him from telling the truth. To no one's surprise he was found guilty. Rather than live in exile for the rest of his life and never to speak in public again, he drank poisonous Hemlock. Although innocent of any crime, he could not live in a political state that considered him a criminal because his thoughts were different.

One of the most famous quotes about suicide is from the philosopher Albert Camus, who wrote during the second world war: *There is but one truly serious philosophical problem, and that is suicide. Judging whether life is or is not worth living amounts to answering the fundamental question of philosophy. All the rest comes afterwards.* This was when Fascists killed around twenty million people for the wrong beliefs or race, and the Communists had killed around sixty million for the wrong thoughts.

In modern times we think we live in a risk-free society. Most people will ask two things when they hear someone has passed away: What did they die of, and how old were they? Older generations may also have the conversation about the wish to die while you can still recognise the people you love rather than spend the last couple of years drugged in a nursing home not knowing your own name. These sorts of conversations invariably end with the belief that quality of life must also include a quality of death, with the idea that you can take your own life if death is close.

But not so much in 1963 it seems. In this respect, Stephen Ward becomes an interesting character. Ward may have been a philanderer and a libertine, but so were most of his rich friends. The trial may have ended his career but certainly not his dream of being an artist. He was fifty years old. He could have gone on the American chat show circuit, he could have written a book, he could have blackmailed numerous people to not write about them and carried on living off his reputation for at least another twenty years. Was there something in his DNA or his history that culminated in his wilful demise. Or did he make that decision as a rational man of medicine, as a stricken artist, a guilty man about to be convicted, or was it circumstances beyond his control that caused him to end his life?

In 1963 you still had capital punishment in England. If you were found guilty of murder, you could be hanged. During this time of "The Cold War" you could also be hanged for treason.

Chapter 2.

Life before The Beatles.

The English criminal justice system goes back hundreds of years. In 1766 the judge William Blackstone stated: *"All presumptive evidence of felony should be admitted cautiously; for the law holds it better ten guilty persons escape than one innocent party suffer."* Blackstone also proposed that all men are innocent until proved guilty. Further to that, the guilt should be proved beyond all reasonable doubt. He also believed that not only should a person be tried by their peers, but unless there are reasons for not doing so, the trial should be held in public. That's a pretty good standard for any country.

What else can we add? The justice system should be that the monarchy, politicians, celebrities and the rich, are not above the law. The right to have legal representation should be available to the defendant from the point of arrest. So strong is this belief that in most countries that today legal representation is free if a person is in police custody. If you are charged with an offence you can apply for aid if you go to court, where you will be entitled to a barrister. The prosecution, the side that acts for the police, will also have a barrister at crown court who will put forward the reasons why the defendant is guilty. Perhaps the most important person in any trial is the judge. They quite often decide what can be said in court, and what can be left out. They can stop proceedings, bring up points of law, and question all those giving evidence. They are looked upon by the jury as the guiding light. So why was there so many miscarriages of justice?

Well, during all this time British justice was run by the establishment. Those in power who told us everyone was equal in the eyes of God, did so from the comfort of their exclusive schools, Oxbridge universities, and country mansions. The key figure which held up the law was religion. You swore an oath on the Bible, but you relied on the belief of people. And people might not be telling the whole truth.

~

Born in Hertfordshire in 1912, Stephen Ward was the son of a vicar whose church was a few miles away from the town of St. Albans. The town was named after a businessman called Alban, who became the first English saint after sheltering Christians from Roman soldiers in what used to be called Verulamium. The Christians were captured, arrested for crimes against the state, and a show trial was planned. The Romans did not know Alban had taken the place of a Christian priest until he stood in front of a judge. The judge was not amused. He decided that if Alban was willing to pretend to be a Christian to let others escape justice, he could be punished like one as well. He was sentenced to death, unless he publicly denounced Christianity. Alban thought about it and chose the morality of silence. The Romans killed him. How much of this martyrdom was instilled on the young Stephen Ward whenever he visited the hallowed ground of St. Albans Cathedral we do not know.

The young Ward was packed off to a half decent boarding school. Here he mixed with the upper echelons of society; something that would have been unthinkable twenty years before. Pubescent schoolboys would have no doubt been enthralled at the scandalous gossip coming out of London. Some of which was created by Tom Driberg; the Anglican churchman, Soviet spy, and Labour politician, would also write about the people making the news, leaving many readers to wonder if there was any difference between those at the top and those at the bottom. Driberg was very much a bottom man. His power and influence were enough that when caught naked in bed with two other men he was acquitted without a stain on his character. His court appearance was not even published in the press.

Ward did not follow in the footsteps of his father once he left school. Nor did he go into some sort of colonial management position still popular in the thirties. Instead, he spent a few years traveling America, where he learnt how to be an Osteopath. The medical profession was another good job for the middle class in these pre-NHS times, although osteopathy was still considered a bit of a quack profession in medicine. There was something about the human body that fascinated him, be it watching, photographing, or simply touching human skin.

Traveling across America, Ward apparently enjoyed the company of prostitutes. He also realised there was no real class division (although this was a country divided by racial lines). No doubt with his well-spoken accent, Christian background, and an ability to soothe aching bones, a man such as Stephen Ward would find himself welcome in all the best brothels.

He was also becoming an excellent portrait artist. Whether it was because his camera was too obtrusive or a way of getting closer to his subjects, or film was too expensive, he was soon bringing women back to study his etchings. Ward could have been a big hit if he had gone to Hollywood or New York. But another war was coming, and he went back to Blighty.

Although he tried to join the armed forces, he was not conscripted until 1942 when he was thirty. Because an osteopath was not considered to be a licensed medical profession, he could not join the Medical Corps. Luckily, whilst in training he met a general who had a bad back. Ward worked his magic and eased the superior officer's pain. Word got around at how good he was, and he then spent most of his training in a little corner of England straightening up the higher ranks, although it should be said that he continued to try and join the medical corps at every opportunity. Towards the end of the war, he got his wish and found himself transferred to India. While there he worked with a doctor who had a practice near Harley Street, who thought he was so good he said Ward should join him in London when it was all over.

Returning home, perhaps the biggest change to post war England was the birth of the National Health Service. Being an osteopath was still quite rare, but GP's could now refer their patients to him. Work ticked along until another stroke of luck. Ward helped an American ambassador with a bad back, who passed on his name to various people, and within a short time Ward was treating numerous dignitaries including the prime minister, Winston Churchill. The greatest ever Englishman was now suffering the slings and arrows of mortality, which put him in need of treatment every week.

Churchill had been quite open about his bouts of depression, which he called his "Black Dog". A dark slouching beast that would follow him for sometimes weeks on end. He once said that when he had it, he would refuse to go on roofs for fear of not being able to stop himself from jumping. But he was lucky in that he knew these dark moods would leave as quickly as they had arrived.

This leads us to an interesting observation of Ward. Both men were talented amateur artists, and no doubt spoke at length on the matter. Both men were passionate by nature and were certainly good talkers (one of the reasons Ward was so popular was because he could tell a good story), but there is nothing to suggest that Ward took advantage of this position. He was the prime minister's osteopath, but he never used it to gain a firmer foothold in the establishment. Most men would have gone straight to the local Freemasons and asked for special treatment. But not Ward. Purely by word of mouth, he ended up treating royalty.

Now heading towards his forties, Ward quickly got married, and then quickly divorced, as she was not so keen on him still wishing to meet other women. In 1950 he became friends with people such as viscount Astor. Bill to his friends, owned Cliveden House, a mansion situated by the river Thames and surrounded by nearly four hundred acres of prime English real estate. The two men became so close that in 1956 Astor gave Ward the keys to a riverside cottage for the doctor to use as his own. On many occasions he would wander up at night to the big house and speak to varied guests such as Prince Philip and the actor Douglas Fairbanks Jnr.

By this time Ward was also moonlighting for a different circle of London society. The showbiz world of theatre and cinema had many stars who suffered from aches and pains. Ward was on hand to heal these patients at all times of the day, even if it meant coming to the theatre or nightclub after dark. For those who enjoyed the baser side of life there were certain other pleasures that also relied on lying on your back, and Ward was just the man for the job.

The people who he met at the theatre, racecourses, the exclusive clubs and restaurants, were all part of the same small clique. For debutantes who had been married off as virgins to someone they met at the Young Conservatives Ball, and the men who didn't want to pay for a prostitute, there was another way of enjoying sex without the pain of divorce. Ward arranged exclusive swingers' parties. He soon realised that many men just wanted to have sex with women while their wives were at home. But where would Ward meet these girls?

A lot of places at the time were membership only clubs merely to get around the strict alcohol licencing laws. If you wanted a drink after hours, you became a member of a club as you walked in. If you had enough money, you joined an official club (usually exclusive by the cost of membership fee), such as Murray's, a cabaret club in Soho, London, which had artistic nude shows almost every night. Again, the strict theatre and performance licensing act forbade any naked dancing or movement. Murrays got around this by having some of the young ladies on stage be topless, but completely still. These artful displays for the men in the audience would be enhanced by skimpily clad women dancing. For Stephen Ward, it was the ideal little drinking oasis in the middle of a cultural desert, because eventually everyone comes to Murrays.

Chapter 3.

A dance to the music of time.

Christine Keeler was born in 1942, near the unfortunately named town of Staines. Her father left the family when she was very young. Later, as a teenager, she was sexually abused on a regular basis by her stepfather and by some of his friends. She fell pregnant at 16 and gave birth, but the baby died. These were the days when sex before marriage was shameful, and abortions were illegal. She ran away to London to work in a café just off Baker Street. A few months later a friend asked her if she wanted to make some real money, and in 1959 she started working in Murrays Cabaret Club as a topless showgirl.

It was here that she met Ward and a friendship was struck. Although the initial encounter would no doubt be Ward asking her to sit at his table and buying her fake champagne, both maintained that they never had sex with each other. I don't know why as both seemed intent on sleeping with as many people as possible. I would like to point out that I am not having a go at Christine, it is really none of our business how many men she slept with; and for that matter we should give Ward the same concession. Although I think that Ward enjoyed watching sex as much as doing it.

Ward saw in Christine someone he could transform into a…I suppose the most apt word in today's world would be "Celebrity". An Eliza Doolittle to his Henry Higgins. At the time *My Fair Lady* was playing in the West End with Rex Harrison and Julie Andrews in the starring roles. It is the story of a rich professor who takes a young waif and turns her into a lady. Perhaps what Ward should have done is look at the personal life of Rex Harrison instead.

For many years Rex had a stormy affair with the actress Carole Landis, until one night she took her own life while he was with her.

For some reason he did not call the ambulance until a long time later. Rumors spread around Hollywood about what had happened, to the point Fox Films cancelled their contract with Harrison shortly afterwards. He spent the next few years on stage until Hollywood asked him to come back. Rex went on the marry the actress Rachel Roberts in 1962, who also went on to commit suicide.

But Ward was not taking Christine to Ascot or getting her to dance with a Lord. In the words of Del Boy, Christine was taken to swingers' parties in large houses where a Duchess had held some magnificent balls in her time. To the Mayfair set, the young Christine had a face that could be deferential and provocative at the same time, as if wearing a French maid's costume while holding a leather whip. No doubt Ward would have loved to have taken a few pictures of that.

When Christine started work at Murray's she not only met Stephen Ward, but also the businessman Peter Rachman. Having escaped from the Nazis during the war, he had made a fortune buying up property all over London and renting rooms out to the newly arrived West Indians. But he was by no means trying to build a socialist utopia. In fact, he was more of a capitalist gangster. He kicked out pensioners who had lived in their homes for years, and let the new arrivals move in at a higher rent (if they could afford it). He must have had some good points, as Christine slept with him that year. This would become a pattern for Christine, finding a fatherly protector rather than a soulmate, and believing that sex came before friendship. She never seemed to be able to grow emotionally from being a teenage girl.

For many, London was still the place where you had to go to achieve fame. Films such as *Expresso Bongo*, released in 1959, featuring a young, mean, and moody Cliff Richard, portrayed Soho as a place that was more steamy than seedy. That was because a lot of film production companies were based in soho, and were never going to let the public know the truth. This led many young girls towards the west end.

Pretty soon Christine was joined by another partner in crime. Mandy Rice-Davies was born in 1944. Her home life seemed to have no outlying problems. Both parents were respectable and could afford to look after a horse for her. While still at school Mandy got a Saturday job and then a modelling job (although she was underage) which took her to London. When she came back home, she knew her future wasn't in Birmingham and ran away as soon as she was sixteen. At that age the police and social services classed you as an adult and so didn't bother looking too hard to find you. Soon she too found herself working at Murrays as a new decade appeared on the horizon.

Murrays Cabaret Club was often seen as the most decadent place in London. It had opened in 1913, just a year after Ward had been born and the music hall tradition was dying. It became a revue bar, where people ate and drank as a show played in the background. During the Second World War it survived on money from American servicemen. It was run by David Murray. With over sixty showgirls in the books, he raised the prices so that only the best (and richest) customers came through the doors.

Mandy forged a letter from her parents to say she was eighteen and became one of the dancers. The girls were paid a basic salary but could earn extra by sitting with the client's in-between shows and getting them to order drinks. They would sip fizzy water passed off as expensive champagne and the customer would be handed an overpriced bill. What the girls did after the club closed was up to them. The trick was knowing which client had lemonade taste and champagne money, and that's where Stephen Ward came in.

When the brunette Christine introduced the blonde Mandy to Ward, he must have thought his black and white dreams had come true. He soon paraded these colourful women among other club members, many of whom were distinguished men of the establishment, such as the conservative Politician John Profumo.

~

John Profumo was born in 1915, just two years older than the future American President John Kennedy. Both had a similar upbringing.

Both came from wealth, although it had taken a while for their families to be accepted by the establishment (the Kennedy's were Catholics in a Protestant country, the Profumo's were Italian in England). Both fathers had been diplomats, both had fallen in love with a German model in the 1930's, and both had a good war record, Kennedy in the far east, Profumo in Europe. Profumo's political career got off to a slow start (he didn't have the help of his father to buy votes), but when the Tories came to power in 1951, he rose steadily up the ranks until by 1959 he was the Secretary of State for Foreign Affairs.

Like Kennedy, Profumo's family life was open to the public. He had married the actress Valerie Hobson, who had been in films such as *Great Expectations*, and *Kind Hearts and Coronets*. While Kennedy was on the campaign trail in the States in 1959, Profumo was celebrating as Harold Macmillan and the Tories won another General Election, possibly keeping them in power until 1964. The constituents of Finchley even voted for a young female conservative called Margaret Thatcher to represent them in parliament.

The aging Harold Macmillan knew it would be his last moments in power, and perhaps the country's as well. He wanted Russia and America to see England as a mediator in world affairs. Unfortunately, the people in power kept having affairs with people who turned out to be spies. One of the first, Klaus Fuchs, had been imprisoned in 1950 for being a spy. He had been handing over atomic secrets since the war to the Russians through a woman with the codename of Sonya. Released in 1959, Klaus promptly fled the country and escaped to East Germany, causing a scandal in the press as to why he had managed to leave so easily? He would not be the last. England seemed better at keeping it up in the bedrooms of Mayfair than the backrooms of the Secret Service. But for the great and the good in the rest of the country it was another occasion where the government had been left with its pants down. What the country needed was a man with political thrust.

After the election Profumo was given the more prestigious job as Secretary of State for War. In such a tense climate between east and west, the name Profumo was constantly in the public eye. When Prime Minister Harold Macmillan, looking considerably old as he gave his "Winds of Change" speech in Colonial Africa, it was no surprise that people looked at Kennedy and began to see Profumo as their own possible "Man of the Decade." Kennedy spoke to America of putting a man on the moon, Macmillan told the English they could all have a washing machine on finance.

But the biggest selling consumer product of 1959 was television. To combat it more films were made in colour than black and white for the first time this year. The nineteen fifties were an austere monochrome period where rationing had only just finished, and teenagers had only just started. The sixties would be one of The Beatles, the Cold War, and the biggest game changer of all…sex.

Chapter 4.

She's in Parties.

How much of your past affects what you say and do in the present? Does what happened to us many years ago have any bearing on the way we behave today? Modern thinking would say that it is vitally important. The past is never over. This brief history of our players helps us to understand the ending. Their journeys are important because in many ways they are a portrayal of the rigid class structure of post-war England at the time. Christine was working class; Mandy was lower middle. Stephen Ward was the epitome of the post-war upper middle-class man. With the right membership to the right clubs and wearing the right tie, he could go anywhere. The problem was he considered himself to be an artist, sort of un-classable, probably the one thing his own social group despised. A doctor was fine, but sketching was a hobby, certainly not something to boast about unless you were talking money.

John Minton was a popular artist in the nineteen fifties. As well as portraits he also did murals and illustrations. No doubt he and Ward would have met at various gallery exhibitions. But by 1956 Minton was out of favour as abstract art dominated everything from kitchenware to the National Gallery. Minton was also a homosexual. He got caught up in a public love triangle and soon found all his friends deserting him. He became depressed and began drinking heavily. In 1957 he took his own life using sleeping tablets. Perhaps there is something else about the past we may have missed.

Everyone you met in the nineteen fifties could have been affected in some way by the war. Post Traumatic stress Disorder has had a lot of names throughout history, such as shell shock; most of them linked to someone suffering or witnessing an extremely distressing situation. A person could be affected weeks, months, even years after the event, creating mental health issues such as anxiety, depression, and erratic behavior such as excessive drinking or gambling. How many were affected we just don't know. People did not want to speak about their mental wellbeing for fear of being placed in the large mental hospitals that circled London and the larger cities. In truth the swinging sixties were not much better. By 1971 Valium was the biggest selling drug in the world.

~

By 1960 Profumo and his wife Valerie Hobson were part of the new "Jet Set". He was popular with the press. She was popular with fans. They were being praised as the new Kennedy's. Perhaps Profumo and JFK were alike in other ways. Neither could help themselves when it came to women. Both were already known to have had a few dalliances already, causing concern among both sets of staff. Both also had global concerns.

    JFK had Vietnam to contend with. There were also the Communists in Eastern Europe, and the Communist Cuban dictatorship on his doorstep. Profumo was the man involved in putting nuclear warheads in missiles (all aimed at Russia). The first nuclear submarine was launched in this year, a sign that Britain was secretly using the "White Heat" of technology before it became a well-known phrase. Both Kennedy and Profumo knew that spying was an effective part of any military intelligence gathering. They were always looking for Russian agents under the bed. Unfortunately, they should have been looking at who was in the bed as well.

    Perhaps it is Stephen Ward who was the one more like Kennedy. Both men had travelled in their youth and had enjoyed the company of numerous women. Both had in interest in the human spine; Ward because it was his work, Kennedy because his back was literally falling apart. The main difference was in their hobbies. Kennedy was a player. He liked sports, sailing, being part of a team, a man who shook hands with everyone. Ward was a watcher. He found solace in drawing, and it certainly became more than just a past time by the late fifties. He had managed to draw the faces of people such as the prime minister Harold Macmillan, and drive to the film studios in Borehamwood to draw Sophia Lauren. In 1960 he had his first exhibition in a London gallery.

Ward had a gift of being able to get important people to sit whilst he drew them. He had drawn most of the royal family, including Thursday Club member Prince Philip, and in this deferential world that would be enough to get through most doors. But he must have had a certain charm, certainly enough to make a good first impression. Ward knew how to tell an interesting story and probably collected them as well.

His technique was to do a couple of basic drawings first, chatting away as he captured images of the face at certain angles and light. He would then do the sitting, which would take less than an hour. The drawing would usually be given to the sitter, with Ward keeping the rough guides. I don't know if he ever did a portrait of himself. Perhaps there was something in his psychological makeup that he didn't want to see, like a man who always takes pictures but never wants his own photograph taken and ends up giving a weak smile when the lens is placed in front of him. He must have had enough charm to be able to draw so many people from the establishment. Although the prime minister would have heard the name of Stephen Ward before then, for other reasons.

In 1956 the Labour politician John Lewis and his wife had been friends with Ward. This was no doubt due to their love of the London night life. Unfortunately, Mrs Lewis began to see less and less of her husband, and filed for a divorce, citing the politicians' sexual peccadilloes as the reason. After one argument, she walked out. Not knowing where to go, she spent the night at Ward's flat. Nothing happened, but John Lewis decided he was going to name Ward as the man who was having an affair with his wife. The politician also claimed that Ward had procured his own wife to give to another friend. Ward, totally innocent, said he would sue for slander. By this time Ward was well known to a few other politicians because of the exclusive parties they attended. Not wanting this sort of thing to be made public, secret meetings took place, and Lewis was told to back down.

But Lewis had friends in the Freemasons and the police. The press called Ward and said that they were going to run a story about him running a vice ring in Mayfair. Ward informed them that if they had no evidence apart from gossip, he would sue. They dropped the story. At the same time the local police were informed that Ward was obtaining girls for wealthy clients. Again, no girl or wealthy client came forward to back up the story, and nothing was done.

Now, Ward had a lot of power regarding the secrets of the rich and famous. What he should have done was stay close with the people with power rather than with the people who liked to party. But Ward was always more bohemian than politician. Whereas President Kennedy made Lyndon Johnson his vice president, a man he had no personal time for, but knew it was a way of obtaining respect and keeping the southern states on his side; Ward continued to form friendships with men because of their shared private passions rather than the public protection they could offer.

If Ward had been found guilty of running a vice ring in 1956 and gone to prison, he would have met some interesting people. Until 1961 suicide was a criminal offence (even the word we still associate with it today, "committed", carries with it the implication that a crime has taken place). On average, people got around three months imprisonment if they were charged with attempting to kill themselves (you wonder if they would have got the death penalty if they had kept trying).

It is doubtful if the prison library would have included Sylvia Plath's first book of poetry, *The Colossus and Other Poems*. Plath suffered from clinical depression from an early age and first tried to kill herself in 1953. She was sent to a psychiatric hospital for six months where she had a range of different therapies, including electric shock treatment. Eventually she returned to college, and in 1956 won a scholarship to Cambridge university in England. Her life as an artist was that of an outsider, never fully being able to join in. She could write about the lives of others, but unable to commit to one herself. Like Ward, both seemed to never want to be inside the frame.

There is something else we should remember. Ward had reached the age when you became someone who was born in a certain decade rather than a certain year; for him it was before The Great War, when men had only just managed to fly across the channel, and now in Ward's lifetime they were talking about putting a man on the moon. I wonder if he began to feel his age over such events, out of step with what's happening around him. There comes a point when we realise we are not young anymore. The clothes feel a little tighter every time you put them on. The supervisors are younger than you, and the music has no meaning. Perhaps he thought that just one more year, maybe two, he would hang up his glory days for quiet nights in his cottage. And then he met a younger version of himself who wanted to taste everything that London had to offer.

The final player in the game is Yevgeny Ivanov. The Soviet Naval Attaché was posted to the Russian Embassy in March 1960. A week later over sixty thousand people marched through the streets of London protesting about American nuclear weapons being based in England. No doubt Ivanov would have been watching. It would be easier to say that everyone at the soviet Embassy was a spy to some degree. Even if you had no training whatsoever you would report everything you saw and heard. That was because there was a real danger that if you did not, someone might accuse you of being a double agent. Again, like Ward, Ivan liked to be on the periphery of events rather than in the middle of them.

Stephen Ward became a minor celebrity in July after his first exhibition of portraits that included royalty, politicians, and celebrities was displayed in a London gallery. The newly arrived diplomat may have attended and believed Ward was a way of getting closer to the establishment. They officially met later that month in The Garrick Club, famous for being full of actors.

Both men may have felt they could gain something out of this relationship. Ivanov would have known about Ward and his parties. If there were photographs of certain people doing private things in Mayfair (or in flagrante), it would give the Communist Party a chance to blackmail half of Whitehall. And things also worked the other way. If Ward was to photograph Ivanov in a compromising position it could be very profitable for the British Secret Service. So, it is strongly possible that Ivanov was also speaking to the KGB, and Ward was speaking to the Secret Service. The loudest whispers in the corridors of power are usually concerned with pillow talk.

PART TWO

They are fully satisfied with their own authority.

1961

Chapter 5.

We're not all going on a Summer Holiday.

We now come to another trial that is relevant to Stephen Ward. In October 1960 began the case of R v Penguin Books in Court No1 of the Old Bailey. It was better known as the Lady Chatterley Trial. Penguin Books wanted to release the unedited edition of the novel *Lady Chatterley's Lover*, which had been written by D. H. Lawrence in 1928 but was later blocked under the Obscene Publications Act (you had to go abroad for an uncut version and smuggle it back). The establishment said No, it was still too rude for the plebs. Penguins' argument was that one could admire the breasts of the Venus De Milo (and Christine Keeler's at Murray's) as they were considered art, but to read about a working-class gardener groping the lady of the manor's was somehow sordid.

John Mervyn Guthrie Griffith-Jones, CBE, was the prosecution barrister. He had been junior counsel for the prosecution against Ruth Ellis. She had been a friend of Ward's, and the last woman to be hanged in the UK. Griffith-Jones told the jury he believed that the novel should remain banned because it induced "*Lustful thoughts in the minds of those who read it*", and "*...When you have read it through, would you approve of your young sons, young daughters – because girls can read as well as boys – reading this book? Is it a book that you would have lying around in your own house? Is it a book that you would even wish your wife or your servants to read?*"

Griffith-Jones believed he was speaking for the "Do as I say, not as I do" brigade. He was a man who had been to Eton and Cambridge; so, the idea of telling trade what to do seemed perfectly natural. More importantly, he believed he had the moral right to speak for (and down to) the general public because he was part of the establishment.

Every trial consist of a fundamental question: Did someone do what is in the definition of the offence they had have been accused of? Every crime is defined by its language, with governments sometimes spending years discussing if a particular word is correct. For example, murder is to *intentionally* kill a person. If you remove the *intent*, someone may still die but it is manslaughter, not murder. To be found guilty, you must fit into every part of the offence within the definition. The prosecution in the Chatterley Trial needed to convince the jury that the work had no artistic merit, and D. H. Lawrence *intended* the novel to be more pornography than literature.

Griffith-Jones was also shocked to find the book contained the C-word on numerous occasions. The C-word was used in the context of a certain part of Lady Chatterley's anatomy (as opposed to saying it after you've just stubbed your toe). The prosecution believed only a select group of people were allowed to say it, and it certainly wasn't the working-class.

The story of Lady Chatterley's Lover was about an affair between the lady of the house and her gardener. Again, another no-no. It was perfectly fine for rich old men to have dalliances with young chamber maids and secretaries, but not the other way around. Griffith-Jones informed the jury that the novel was filled with detailed acts of sexual intercourse. The right honourable barrister believed that such things could be spoken about at his gentleman's club but not found on the shelf in a local branch of W. H. Smiths for any woman to devour.

At this point the judge made the decision that perhaps the jury should read the book first before deciding if it had any literary merit, or, under the definition of the law, it was obscene. The jury quickly went away to see what all the fuss was about. Once the climax was over, Griffith-Jones started again.

But in some ways, he had already overplayed his hand. He said that the story and the language used made it obscene. But to prove it he had to say those words, taking away some of their power.

The defence argued the book was a work of art and should be considered on literary merit. To ban it would be tantamount to putting a pair of underpants on the statue of David. The book also had the advantage of, A: Only being dangerous to those members of the public who could read. And surely it was reading that elevated the mind and spirit to higher purposes. B: As well as the content, one would also have to understand the intent of the author (and in so doing, the mind of the reader). In other words, the book was only sinful to those who already had a knowledge of sin themselves. How could you corrupt those who already had carnal desires?

After a week of debating the jury decided that certain words, although offensive, could be heard anywhere, even by people who did not know how to read or write. Within the definition of The Obscene Publications Act, D. H. Lawrence did not intend to write something pornographic; rather, he was using language in its most primal sense. There was also the issue that once you start cancelling freedom of speech you eventually turn into the rabid fascist or communist fanatic that you originally opposed. Thanks to the direction of the judge the Jury made the right decision and said the book was not obscene. when the novel was released for publication, it sold two hundred thousand copies on its first day.

Chapter 6.

Casino Royal.

In 1961 the army of children born after 1945 would soon be leaving school. They were the first generation raised on television and transistor radios. For them there would be no hiding from the blitz, no national service, no turning into their parents. Sex was about to become far more open than at any time since the Romans. If the 1950s was a formal suit, the 1960s would be a birthday one.

Stephen Ward was facing the prospect of turning fifty. He should have grown old gracefully, instead he was spending every evening with Christine and Mandy at Murray's, eventually sleeping with Mandy. At the time Christine was sleeping with millionaire slum landlord Peter Rachman, but at some point, she stopped, and Mandy took over. The say that "power corrupts, and absolute power corrupts absolutely." I used to believe that quote was about the person who had the power, but now I think it also relates to those around them. In the world of sexual politics this was capitalism with a large C.

For a few the good times of the fifties continued into the next decade. Enter Mariella Novotny. In her twenties, she had married antiques dealer Horace Dibben, a gregarious portly pervert of heroic proportions and nearly forty years older than her. Along with Ward, they organised parties in Mayfair which included the infamous orgy where a man (allegedly a high-up member of the establishment) wore a mask, a small (masonic) apron, and a sign around his neck that if his services were not up to standard you had permission to cane him. Rumours abounded that it was a member of parliament, or even royalty. This was also the party where Mandy said that when she arrived late Ward opened the door wearing nothing but a pair of socks. Horace Dibben was busy watching his wife take on six men.

Horace Dibben's other passions included golf, antiques, and sado-masochism (he was unlucky there, as golf isn't too popular in Hertfordshire). Over time he became more interested in watching sex than doing it. He and Ward had a mutual friend in George Harrison-Marks, who lived in Ewhurst Manor in Borehamwood, near Elstree Film Studios. Harrison-Marks liked to make his own films. These were naughty "Stag Do" reels, tame by today's standards, but arrestable all those years ago. Harrison-Marks also took pictures for magazines. These included naturist type pics and specific images such as naughty schoolgirls caning innocent businessmen. Under the obscene publications act you couldn't show much in England, but in Europe you could. So, you would double your money with the one photo shoot and take twice as many pictures, sending the soft-core stuff to Soho and the hard core to Sweden. Ward would often travel down to Borehamwood to the house behind Whitehouse Farm with one or two girls for Harrison-Marks to photograph. Ward, also a keen photographer, no doubt took a few pictures himself.

It was through Harrison-Marks that Ward had met viscount Bill Astor. Ward continued to remain close to people such as Harrison-Marks and Dibben years later. He would often see a pretty woman in London, see if she was into a certain lifestyle, take her to Borehamwood for pictures, and invite her to parties. Sometimes they would become starlets, while other times…

Diana Doors, who would later tell stories of parties at her home where people would secretly watch others having sex through a two-way mirror in the ceiling, remembers meeting Ward, who at the time was enjoying the company of his escort Ruth Ellis, and found him slightly pompous. Perhaps Ward only liked the thrill of seeing people in power parading naked.

The Hod Dibben parties were legendary and very exclusive. Mariella Novotny claimed to be East European royalty and expected to be sired by men within her orbit, both socially and literally. There were rumours that Prince Philip had attended some of these parties. Any photographs of his indiscretion would be highly valuable. And Mariella always liked to aim high. She was to later to go to New York around the same time as Christine and Mandy, where she possibly helped President Kennedy ride out his bad back. But that is the future. What we have at the moment are parties organised by Ward, who could have also been taking pictures.

    The same time these infamous parties were taking place, a man called Peter Llewelyn Davies walked through the streets of London. Now in his sixties, he was the inspiration for Peter Pan, the boy who never grew up. Like Ward, he too fought in the war, which for him was The Great War. He too had been hospitalised. For the rest of his life, he seemed to remain a Lost Boy, seemingly enjoying life, but never being able to settle down. He walked through Chelsea to Sloane Square underground station. Waiting on the platform, he jumped down onto the tracks as the tube train came out of the tunnel. The coroner reported that he had killed himself "while the balance of his mind was disturbed". This is language to get Llewelyn Davies buried in a church, as some still refused to give suicide victims a Christian burial.

    For Ward, the cottage in Cliveden was a type of Neverland. It allowed him to leave the past behind and draw pictures of a boat on a river.

~

A group who now called themselves *The Beatles* returned from Hamburg and began to play at the Cavern Club in Liverpool. The female contraceptive pill had reached the final testing stage and would soon be available on prescription (but only to married women). On television a new show called The Avengers started a run that would last until the end of the decade. Patrick Macnee played the gentleman agent in the suit and bowler hat whilst Honour Blackman was his attractive partner. The writers changed the female character every couple of years for a younger model. Fictional spying was sexy. Real spies such as those involved in the Portland Spy Ring were not.

In 1959 the CIA passed on information that the Russians were getting secrets about British Naval Intelligence from a base in Portland, England, which housed the nuclear submarine project. Two members of staff, Harry Houghton and Ethel Gee, were stealing top secret details and taking them to London. There they would meet a jukebox salesman called Gordon Lonsdale. MI5 were informed and decided to put Lonsdale under surveillance. He would take regular journeys to Ruislip, to meet a genteel old couple called Mr and Mrs Kroger, antique book dealers who worked from their little semi-detached suburban home.

All five people were arrested after equipment used to turn photographs into microdots were found in the address. These would then be put into the spines of books and sent abroad. All five were given double figure prison sentences. But there was a bigger shock than an ordinary suburban couple being traitors. It turned out that the CIA had passed on their intelligence to the British in 1956, but the government failed to act on the information for five years. This was truly scandalous. It then turned out that Mr and Mrs Kroger were in fact Morris and Lona Cohen, American spies who had worked with Ethel and Julius Rosenberg before they had been executed in 1953. Worse, it later transpired that Gordon Lonsdale was in fact Konon Molody, a KGB agent who had been operating in England for the last few years seemingly without MI5's knowledge. The press demanded answers. In politics the situation would best be described as a complete fuck-up. How did the establishment make such a series of calamitous mistakes? There were rumours that people higher up in both admiralty and government had been coerced into keeping quiet, although nothing was made public. Between 1955 and 1959 the First Sea Lord was Louis Mountbatten, who would have known Ward from The Thursday Club. The married Mountbatten was rumoured to be into bisexual orgies.

George Blake worked for MI6. He was also working for the communist party at the same time. In 1956 he was in Berlin trying to recruit soviets into becoming double agents. He also handed over details of British spies to his communist bosses. It is believed at least forty people were compromised over the next six years: with some even being executed. Blake was only caught when a soviet agent defected and promptly informed the British that one of their own was also one of Russia's best spies. Just like all the other times there were also rumours that the establishment had been aware of the situation and had done nothing.

Blake was arrested for treason in 1961. His trial as it was held in secret. It must have been bad as the judge gave him 42 years. Bizarrely, a short time later he somehow escaped from the high security prison of Wormwood Scrubs and managed to get all the way to East Germany, where the Communist Party publicly congratulated him. What details were said in court, and how he escaped without getting caught, remains a mystery.

Chapter 7.

The banality of fame.

It is believed that four out of ten men will suffer some form of mental illness in their lives. If you lined up the social classes in order, from a tramp at one end to a multi-millionaire at the other, you would not be able to pick out which four men are the most likely to be struck down with it. Stephen Fry, an extremely talented and overall nice man attempted to take his own life in 2013. He was in his fifties, loved by the public, and had over thirty years of a great career. He put it down to a combination of the type of Bi-Polar that he has and his personal circumstances at the time which all seemed to come together to create the perfect storm. Which makes me wonder that if he can be vulnerable, what about Stephen Ward?

Again, who knows how much people are affected by their past. Ward was involved in an incident in India during the war. It is not clear what that was, but he received hospital treatment for it. Ward was effectively shipped home, and his conscription was ended for medical reasons.

When he moved to London there is another story that has a bearing on his future. Ward fell in love. For whatever reason it didn't work out, and she left him. A friend recalled that Ward tried to kill himself by taking an overdose, and the friend administered treatment to wake him up. Knowing that this information was only reported after his death makes it difficult to say how accurate it is, especially as there is no date to when it happened apart from possibly the very early fifties. But if true it now puts Ward in a new light. There is no record of him seeking any medical help; but then how many men today also get close to taking their own life, and afterwards simply carry on as if nothing had happened?

Ward certainly wasn't poor. There was the medical practice near Baker Street and his reputation as a portrait artist that now included eight members of the royal family among his subjects. Stephen Fry said that for most of his life he had to hide his sexuality. For Stephen Ward it was a case of keeping his own sexual proclivities secret. He liked to watch people having sex. In a world before the web had widened to allow individuals to look at porn anywhere and anytime, Ward found himself surrounded by people forced to share the same sinful secret. But the problem with every addiction is that you keep having to raise the dosage.

By now he had met Yevgeny Ivanov and had been in contact with a man in the Secret Service who had the codename of "Woods". Here was a chance for Ward to finally say he had done something for his country. He had the tailored suits, the fast car, and the girls. Being James Bond might give his life the meaning he had been searching for. The only problem was that this was not fiction. When it comes to real life, not everyone thinks you are the hero of the story.

~

The July weekend at Cliveden in 1961 is seen was the start of Ward's downfall, but is that really the case? Yevgeny Ivanov would have been fully aware of what part he was going to play whilst in England. As a Russian, people would approach him for three reasons: One, to see if he was trying to defect. Two, if he was willing to become a double agent. Three, if he could be blackmailed into passing on Soviet secrets. The easiest way to catch a spy was not what was in their political manifestos, but what was in their pants.

The honeytrap called for an attractive female (or male) who was able to get the person in bed. An older man wanting to do anything for a younger woman has been going on since King Herod. Take them to an address where the bedroom has a two-way mirror and get them to perform while the person films them in the next room. After a couple of photographs of them getting a happy ending you had the start of a new relationship. Of course, the Russians also knew how it worked (probably better). They would play along trying to find out who else was involved, no doubt hoping to get some information themselves. The communists knew all about Dr Stephen Ward, and that he was friends with the Secretary of State for War John Profumo. A man who liked to party like Yevgeny Ivanov would be the ideal person to find out if Profumo was planning on letting the Yanks store some of their nuclear warheads on British missiles.

The friendship between Ward and Ivanov had been going on about a year before the night of Cliveden. Ward treated Ivanov as if he was one of his young starlets, taking him to numerous parties, enjoying the thrill of frisson in the political tension when placing a red in the room. Although not everyone was pleased to see a real communist in the flesh. This included the bizarre scene one night in 1960 with Ivanov and the actor Paul Carpenter, whose credits include The *Sea Shall Not Have Them* and *Goldfinger*, when they started arguing about communism. It ended in a scuffle, with Ward, and of all people, Sid James (of the Carry-On films), having to break them apart. Also at the party was Christine Keeler.

MI5 and MI6 would certainly have taken an interest in who Ivanov was talking to. Stephen Ward would have been top of the list. The concern with Ward was the people he partied with. If the name of Christine Keeler was also on file, it was essentially as one of Ward's escorts.

A few years later when Ward tried to tell people that the Secret Service had been in touch with him a year before Cliveden, they called him a liar and a fantasist, but it was all true. But if it ever came out that MI5 were employing him for their services (a man who liked to watch women being serviced by other men), the British government would look like fools. As for Christine Keeler, the truth was that she simply wasn't clever enough to be a honeytrap.

Ward said there was a lunch between him and the man from MI5 codenamed "Woods" on 8th June 1961, a month before Profumo and Ivanov were to meet at Cliveden House. Unfortunately, the full details of this discussion are still secret today. Around twenty years after

Ward's death an official MI5 report was released which recorded that there was a meeting where Ward came forward after the Cliveden weekend with information that Ivanov and Profumo had met and offered to help the government in any way but was politely turned down.

The government are clearly lying. Let's start with the obvious, who arranged these meetings? It couldn't have been Ward as you can't just pop into the Secret Service and have a chat. If it was the government that orchestrated any of the meetings, when did they target Ward, who organised it, why only after Cliveden, and what did they expect to get out of him?

Ward did speak to MI5 again sometime after Cliveden, so at least we have a half truth. And in that case why did no one from the Secret Service come forward at Ward's trial? The answer lies in the fact that Ward was never on trial for anything that happened at Cliveden, although once charged both he and Christine were unable to talk about it for legal reasons. Ironically, a film was in production which gave some idea of what Ward was to later face.

Franz Kafka's *The Trial* is the story of a man arrested and put on trial for an offence he knows nothing about. His friends and acquaintances all desert him. The investigation takes months before anything happens. When he is finally put in the dock the courtroom is filled with people he does not know. At some point the man is not even sure that the trial is over, but the sense of an ending hangs over him. The establishment orders him to take his own life to resolve their problem. He doesn't, so they kill him and make it look like suicide.

For Stephen Ward 1961 must have seemed like a very good year. But circumstances beyond his control were now moving inexorably closer towards that perfect storm when the police would knock on the door two years later.

Chapter 8.

Picture yourself on a Boat on a River

To Kill a Mockingbird was published in 1960 and a film followed a few years later. For a while there seemed to be a lot of films about people being judged for a crime they had not committed. No doubt a lot of this stemmed from the real-life McCarthy witch hunts for communists in America that had appeared in the newsreels a few years earlier. But there was also another trial that ended up being watched by millions, this time on television.

On 11th April 1961 the trial of Adolf Eichmann started. This was the first trial that was televised and shown around the world. The former high-ranking Nazi had been illegally smuggled out of South America and bought to Israel and then charged with the offence of Crimes against Humanity. Eichmann's defence was that he did not physically kill anyone; he was following the orders of his government, which if he had disobeyed, he himself would have been sent to a camp.

As a young man he joined a political party which had won a democratic election. The Third Reich only became a dictatorship once it was in power. It did this by creating a series of emergencies in which it was able to take away the rights of individuals until the government even controlled their thoughts. Eichmann had no say in any of this agenda. He was working within state rules before the war had started and had not committed any criminal offence. When war broke out, just like every other country involved, the rules changed. Dropping bombs on hundreds of women and children was considered heroic. The value of a human life was thrown out in order to keep the value of an idea alive. After a series of winning battles Eichmann was put in charge of deporting all Jews out of Germany.

Within another few years the Nazis began to lose. Eichmann was ordered to make decisions which he knew would lead to the death of others. Eichmann may have thought that this was no different from an American deciding to bomb Berlin, or a British captain sinking a cargo ship. Although I would argue that there is a clear difference (one side was fighting for democracy). It didn't matter. It is always the victors who get to decide what was right and what was wrong.

The defendant was a man seemingly without friends, for no German was going to come forward to give evidence and then be asked questions about their own past. The defence argued that his actions were immoral rather than unlawful, and that the victors were merely trying to use the holocaust to justify their own acts such as dropping the atomic bomb. It is believed Fascism killed about thirty million people during its reign, Communism had killed a hundred million (and still counting in 1961), the Allies killed about three million (and still counting if you added the high cancer rate in Japan).

But the judge pointed out that the offence of "Crimes against humanity" was first used by the Abraham Lincoln administration in 1860 when discussing the slave trade. It became international law in 1915. As such, the Nazis should have been aware the holocaust was illegal under international law.

Eichmann then changed his defence. He argued a point of law that was true in 1961 and still is today. Israel was bound by the same set of judicial laws as England and America: That there should be enough evidence to charge the defendant of a criminal offence and bring him to court, that the trial should be open and fair unless there are issues of national security, and that the burden of proof is that the person is guilty beyond all reasonable doubt. Finally, the trial should take place in the country where you committed the offence. Eichmann should have been tried in Germany. Israel got around this by having three judges, one of which was German and had lived in Germany during the Third Reich. It would seem the establishment wanted to win no matter what. Were they right to do this, probably. Was it legal, probably not.

During the trial, one of the watchers sat in the gallery was Stephen Ward. He had been sent to sketch the proceedings by Colin Hoote, editor of the Daily Telegraph. Although it was being televised, the court drawings would be published in newspapers. Footage of the holocaust was shown during the trial. Even now the images of naked men and women waiting to die are still extremely disturbing. Ward the artist, the doctor, the libertine, would not have been able to look away. And as an educated man, he must have wondered how those in power managed to conceal such a bright shining lie.

Eichmann was more than just a man taking orders, he was there at the Wannsee conference in 1942 when it was decided the number of Jews captured was so high it was simply impossible to imprison or deport them all. At that conference the final solution was decided. Eichmann may have felt that to oppose the idea would mean death for him and his family and so went along with it. He could well be right. We all like to think that we would be on the right side of history, but the reality is most of us would rather spend our lives squatting in quiet desperation than make a stand.

And what did Ward think of all this as he drew the man accused of such terrible crimes? The world had progressed from killing six million Jews over several years to having the capability of killing millions of people within a couple of seconds. Eichmann, who started off as a man filled with good intentions, had somehow ended up on a road to hell. The only thing he had been allowed to keep from his past were an old pair of glasses he wore in the dock.

~

I sometimes wonder if you ever really get away with committing a crime. You may not know the legal definition of the offence, but there is always the worry that you might be caught. It doesn't have to be by the police, it could be your family, friends or even your own soul that eventually puts you on trial. Raskolnikov in *Crime and Punishment* believed that if committing a crime made the world a better place, then it was not really a crime. But his conscience judged otherwise.

And if Eichmann knew what the outcome would be from the moment war started, or he agreed to the final solution in 1942, or even when he was arrested, why did he not try to take his own life? Perhaps part of him believed he was innocent in the eyes of the law. Ward finished his pictures and flew back before Eichmann was sentenced to death. Perhaps there are some things where the outcome is inevitable no matter what you say or do.

The book Ward may have chosen to read on the plane was *The Old Man and the Sea*. The writer Ernest Hemmingway had other passions, mainly drinking. But this was the nineteen-fifties; everybody drank. The real problem was when you tried to stop drinking and realised you couldn't.

That's the thing with addiction; they are a chance to escape reality, but life tends to bite back. Suffering from high blood pressure and chronic pain, Hemmingway had been using alcohol and various legal medications for many years. On 2nd July 1961 he shot himself in the head rather than live another day. The man who had won the Nobel prize for literature with his short brisk writing style didn't leave any famous last words. The man who had tried to cut out all the bullshit in his novels had also decided to do it with his life. His death made the headlines at the start of July 1961, by then Stephen Ward had already planned to spend the weekend with a group of friends at Cliveden. Who needed *The Old Man and the Sea* when you would be with a young woman by a swimming pool.

Chapter 9.

Sex and drugs and Vodka Stolle.

On a sunny warm weekend in 1961 Stephen Ward, Christine Keeler, and others including a woman called Sally Norie, were staying in the cottage on the Cliveden estate. They would soon meet both Secretary of State for War John Profumo and his wife. Later, USSR Naval Attaché Yevgeny Ivanov would join the distinguished guests. Whether he had been to the cottage before is not known. Viscount Astor would no doubt enjoy his company. Unlike some of the film and TV series based on the scandal, Astor was no bumbling imbecile. During the war he was a British naval intelligence officer and had spent thirty years in professional politics. It was only his father dying that made him give up a career in Westminster.

On Saturday night the president of Pakistan talked about the hot weather to the Profumo's in Cliveden's large dining room, while Ward and his group of friends went up to use the swimming pool for a dip. Christine had taken off her costume and was doing the breaststroke (all in the best possible taste). When she got out, Jack Profumo appeared in his tuxedo and offered her a towel.

The next day Astor and his friends spent the day by the pool along with Ward and his group, where they were joined by Yevgeny Ivanov. Again, the story goes that Christine now made an impression on the Russian. Although Ward had his camera and took a few pictures, strangely, no one can remember if Profumo and Ivanov ever got the chance to speak to each other. Instead, games were played in the pool, with Profumo cheating in a piggyback race. Although he was in company with his wife, later that day Profumo made it clear to Ward that he wanted to see Christine again. He must have been a bit jealous when Christine needed to get back to London and Ivanov offered her a ride.

Allegedly, as we only have Christine's version given to a journalist, when they went back to London, Ivanov opened a bottle of Vodka, and they had sex. If they did, I am pretty sure Ivanov only saw Christine as a good time girl and not some Mata Hari secret agent. We should also say that Christine wasn't planning on getting Profumo in the sack to see what secrets he would disclose.

As for Stephen Ward, he knew about Ivanov and Christine because Christine told him. He also knew that Profumo wanted to meet with her as well because Profumo had told him. Little wonder that on 12th July 1961, Ward reported on the weekend's events to MI5. He told an agent named Woods that Ivanov and Profumo had met and at Cliveden and had shown considerable interest in Christine. Ward also stated that he had been asked by Ivanov that weekend for information about the future arming of West Germany with nuclear warheads.

At this stage Profumo had not slept with Christine. That meant the meeting was all about Ivanov. But why would Ward know about military secrets? Something is clearly missing in this account. Because of Profumo's position (in Government), his name (and that of Christine) was handed to MI5's director-general, Sir Roger Hollis. In that summer of sixty-one he probably knew of Ward due to the parties.

But let's also look at the relationship between Ward and Profumo. Ward must have known the Secretary of State for War for quite a while for the politician to tell an osteopath that he wanted to have sex with Christine and had no worries about Ward getting upset or blackmailing him. Both men had been part of the London scene for nearly ten years, and it is highly likely they frequented the same social functions along others in the establishment. But this is still a big ask. Their relationship would have to be very tight for Profumo to let his intentions be known at Cliveden. Perhaps they had met at one of Ward's other parties?

The fifties are seen as the age of prim and proper, but some members of the establishment were certainly swinging before the sixties started. The first instamatic, or hidden camera, appeared during the Duchess of Argyll scandal when she was photographed giving a blowjob to someone who was not her husband. There are stories of Ward spending nights chatting half naked to various guests rather than joining in with the orgy. He was probably one of the first to suffer the malaise of modern man: the banality of porn. By the time we reached the summer of sixty-one, while Profumo and Ivanov were groping the same woman, Ward had pictured himself doing the job of servicing secrets.

~

In the month when everyone met at Cliveden, you had Princess Diana being born, and Khrushchev warning the British ambassador that England should stay out of West Berlin otherwise, he would be quite willing to use Hydrogen bombs on London. In August Barrack Obama was born, and the Berlin Wall went up, effectively cutting the city in half. September saw Russia openly carry out military manoeuvres while the world watched (and did nothing). October had the first edition of Private Eye, the satirical magazine formed in part by Peter Cook. You also have the first stand-off at Checkpoint Charlie between Russian and American tanks.

In November President Kennedy sent 18,000 "military advisors" to South Vietnam. This effectively rules out escalating the conflict in Europe. Those early years in the far east allowed America to flex its military muscles and show Russia it was willing to put boots on the ground if it needed to. Thanks to America's refusal to help Britain during the Suez Crisis the British now did the same to America in Vietnam. This bit of petulance would later turn out to be one of the greatest things Macmillan's Conservative party ever did.

And during all this activity there would have been conversations taking place between Ward and Ivanov, Ward and the MI5 agent

"Woods", perhaps even Ward and Profumo, no doubt Keller somewhere in the middle. Ward was still having his parties in Mayfair, his trips to Borehamwood, and weekends in the cottage by the river. No doubt he would have been accompanied by various women, although a few years later the police did not seem that bothered to try and trace who these women were. They had all the people they wanted already in the frame.

Chapter 10.

It was over twenty years ago today.

In 1957 the Wolfenden Report concluded that Homosexual acts carried out in private between men over twenty-one should be made legal (lesbians were not a problem). The government agreed in principle but didn't want the idea rammed down the public's throat, so it remained illegal until 1967. In the meantime, just growing your hair longer than the usual short back and sides somehow casted aspersions on your masculinity. What was worse, the young seemed to be forgetting who won the bloody war anyway. A sexual revolution was happening, and the older generation had no idea how to stop it.

By 1961 American culture had truly taken over the hearts and minds of the young. Everything about the country seemed new. They had turned capitalism into pop consumerism and sharp suited conservatism. The best television shows were American. They had the cars, the girls and the guns. Every show would end with the bad guy losing and the good guy riding off into the sunset. Every news report showed President Kennedy promising to take us to the moon.

The problem was that the communists kept changing the script. Yuri Gagarin became the first man in space rather than John Glenn. The Russian toured England to amazed crowds, meeting Prince Philip and Stephen Ward at a party held in his honour. Many must have wondered how an oppressive ideology was winning the space race. The answer was simple: They must have cheated.

Whilst our spies were elegant with a touch of integrity and only did what they had to do in order to save the free world, the communist spies were sneaky backstabbers who would steal all our hard-earned secrets in order to dominate us. The truth about our league of gentlemen spies was that by the nineteen-sixties most of them were already in their fifties. The cold war was starting just as they were going to bed. Parliament, Whitehall, and the Secret Service was still a place where the right school and university was more important than such a thing as talent. It wasn't so much incompetence that was defeating the British intelligence systems time after time, it was a form of class segregation and the belief that someone wearing the same patterned tie could never be anything but honest.

Stephen Ward and Christine Keeler were still living together at his Mews flat in London. Their relationship was purely platonic, although for some reason he had slept with Mandy Rice-Davies. Of everything written about Christine and Mandy, it is the younger blonde who appears to be the real political animal and the one who would have made a good honey trap. But politicians and diplomats were as tight with money then as they are now. Little wonder that Mandy decided to stay with the millionaire slum landlord Peter Rachman than spend the weekend in a grotty cottage by the river.

By autumn Christine had officially finished with Profumo and Ivanov and was a free agent. She tried modelling and acting, but with little success. She dated other men, but nothing serious. To put it simply, she was a woman in her early twenties who was hanging about with men in their fifties and needed a bit more excitement in her life. Part of that was moving to a flat in Dolphin Square, a large block of flats overlooking the Thames at Pimlico, where she could entertain friends.

Dolphin Square was also used by a lot of politicians and civil servants such as John Vassall. He also liked to have parties, although they tend to be a men only affair. How Christine could afford such a desired residence I'm not sure. Perhaps she was still entertaining friends in high places.

In the early sixties people had no idea about drugs. They drank like fish and smoked like chimneys no problem, but anything else above laxative chocolate was dangerous. The birth control pill was contested in parliament for fear that its release on to the general public would reduce the morals of society and turn women into sexual maniacs. This was the same parliament who knew their own politicians were having sex with as many different people as possible in private.

    In fiction, illegal drugs, like illegal sex, were morality lessons. The parties were always fun at the start while everyone was getting high, but someone was always going to come down hard. Men would lose their social standing; women would end up walking the streets. In the nineteen-forties the government was happy for people to use their drugs throughout the war, mostly amphetamine type pills to keep soldiers and civilians awake. In the fifties other drugs such as heroin and cocaine were still available on prescription, seemed to be for the more artistic types. The aristocrats seemed to enjoy it; on the basis they didn't have to get up for work the next day. Cannabis, which was believed to have been in England in Shakespeare's time, now returned with the Windrush generation, but the British Government didn't want an encore.

    The story of how cannabis became illegal is an interesting one. At the start of the last century America became concerned about the influx of Mexican migrants. Not only did these darker skinned people have strange customs and music, but they also liked to smoke hemp. Because it grew in the wild, it was impossible to tax. Local laws were passed in the southern states to keep the Mexicans in check. You couldn't stop the weed from growing but you could stop it from being smoked. In reality no one really cared as long as the Mexicans kept working. Then in the nineteen-twenties the multi-millionaire Randolph Hearst became one of the main players to make sure it was prohibited from being bought or sold throughout the country. He owned numerous newspapers all over America, selling over forty million copies a day. He also owned numerous pulp and paper factories near logging mills, allowing him to cut down hundreds of trees a day. Other countries such as Mexico and Jamaica could produce hemp far quicker than trees, turning the stalks into pulp and selling the cheaper paper to his rivals. Hearst bribed the Senate to ban hemp through its Trading

Standards Laws, both its pulped version and its leaves. It was deemed unclassifiable under the Trades Description Act (unlike tobacco), and any country that tried export it was likely to face tough sanctions by the ever-growing American economy. There's more. Hearst was also a good old-fashioned racist. He believed that Mexicans and blacks were particularly fond of the stuff and so went out of his way to publicise how dangerous cannabis was in the newspapers he owned.

In England those from the west-Indies brought with them the idea that cannabis was no different to alcohol. But it was the colour of their skin rather than the skinning up that seemed to upset the establishment. Drugs became linked with blacks, which became linked to crime. As immigration went up in the sixties the government and the police cracked down. This was still the case years later. In the early eighties Rodney from *Only Fools and Horses* was given a £250 fine (nearly a thousand pounds today) and two years suspended sentence just for smoking a "Jamaican Woodbine".

We know that in the summer, Ward took Christine to an all-night café in Notting Hill to score some cannabis, and it is here she met Aloysius "Lucky" Gordon. Being seen with Lucky Gordon was extremely dangerous in the early 60's. Inter-racial relationships were not well received by the locals. At thirty years old, he was more her age than previous men. Lucky also had a bit of a temper. It was a pity Christine had found someone who had more in common with Sugar Ray Robinson than Smokey Robinson. It's possible her London flat had become a place where the rich could obtain whatever drug of choice they wanted. Which also meant Christine was trapped in an abusive relationship which she could not financially escape from. She tried to leave him a few times; but he kept coming back. During this time Christine also began to distance herself from Ward and Mandy.

Christine and Mandy had been young women intent on having a good time in London. Again, our modern morals may say So What? You could argue that no one held them against their will and forced them to party with rich older men. How many women are doing that in Dubai right now? But there is one thing that makes me uneasy about their situation: their age. Mandy was still only seventeen in 1961; Christine was just two years older. Lucky Gordon was thirty when he met Christine, and slum landlord Peter Rachman was forty-one when he had met Mandy. It appears the girl's had taken flight to London only to end up as caged birds.

Peter Rachman is certainly an interesting character. A Polish Jew who had been in a concentration camp, only to escape and put in a Russian detention camp until the Nazis invaded. He then became part of the Polish resistance. He escaped and became a British citizen in 1948. Working for an estate agent, within ten years he had a built up a property empire of his own. Using the methods he had learnt during the war to gazump his rivals, he advanced over parts of Nothing Hill and West London by moving protected tenants into smaller buildings, then turning the large houses into flats and putting in Jamaican immigrants. Now this may look like quite an altruistic thing to do; but in truth Rachman was charging his black tenants more rent than white ones.

In 1959 the police tried to get Rachman on numerous charges, including demanding money with menaces and fraud; but Rachman was a director of so many companies that it was impossible to keep track of where the money had gone. He was also rich enough to stay out of court and the newspapers, although sometimes you needed a bit more protection than was legal.

In 1960 he got the Krays to help on the doors of a couple of nightclubs he owned. As one of them was as mad as a box of frogs with a stare that looked as if he was either going to fight you or fuck you (or probably both), Rachman soon realised he could end up being buried in the concrete of one of his building sites if he didn't make Ronnie happy. The twins eventually took over one of his clubs in Knightsbridge in return to leave him alone. Rachman decided he needed his own henchmen working for him, such as Johnny Edgecombe and Michael de Freitas.

De Freitas was portrayed in the film *The Bank Job* as a British Malcolm X, a man who wanted justice for the black community. But again, the truth was slightly different. De Freitas was a drug dealing pimp and thug who was employed to beat the shit out of black men and women if they didn't pay on time. Rachman used him to run the brothels in the buildings he owned, often making films and photographs of the working women as they worked (and were worked over).

Rachman continued to make money and keep Mandy as his mistress in his Mews flat while his wife lived in his house in Hampstead. When he died suddenly in 1961, he was buried at Bushey Jewish cemetery, just five minutes away from Borehamwood. Mandy was distraught and attempted to commit suicide by taking pills. It was Stephen Ward who came to her aid and then let her recover in his flat. He even let her parents stay for a few weeks until she felt better. She resumed her friendship with Christine, who was still being abused by Lucky Gordon.

He was later arrested by the police for assault, but Christine dropped the charges. If she had only had the strength to have given evidence on this first occasion things might have been so much different. As for Ward, he seemed to have met a few women throughout 1961, but they never turned into anything serious.

His relationships were like his art, portraits of faces but never a full-bodied commitment. There may be a flip side to this in that the women he met found it impossible to love a man who could never let go of his addictions. Ward was an artist cursed by an imagination that would never let him give up the ghost.

PART THREE

Never make a defence or apology

before you be accused.

1962

Chapter 11.

That was the year that was.

In January we have the first ever record from The Beatles with the song *My Bonnie*. Although for the moment they were the backing group for *Tony Sheridan*, for the record they were called *the Beat Brothers*. In February *The Sunday Times* produced its first colour supplement. Papers such as *The Sunday Times, The News of the World*, and *The People*, sold in their millions. So much so, they could afford to pay thousands of pounds for a story. Their only fear were threats of libel. If they printed something which a judge believed to be a lie they could be sued for hundreds of thousands of pounds. They would often get around this by slightly changing names.

Ward met with agent Woods again. Ward would later tell people that Woods wanted information on Ivanov. They also wanted Ward to pass on selective information to the Russian, knowing it would get back to his superiors, just to see how well thought of he was as a spy. How much Ward spoke about Profumo and Christine, we don't know.

In June, The Beatles went down to London and record some songs at Abbey Road Studios. This was their last chance of making it. Another failure and they were going to pack it all in. Imagine how different the sixties would have been if John Lennon had gone off and become a postman. A few weeks later a group called The Rolling stones played their first show at the Marquee Club in Soho. Within twelve months both bands would be selling millions of records and filling newspaper headlines on a regular basis.

Queen Magazine, which was a sort of posh periodical that focused mainly on the younger members of the establishment and the Chelsea jet set, was popular in London. The owners went on to finance the pirate station Radio Caroline before the magazine was eventually given the new name of *Harpers Bazaar*. Among its regular articles was a little piece called *Sentences I'd like to hear the end of*. These would often be used to spread a rumour without getting caught in the strict libel laws. The July 1962 edition it hinted of a possible political triangle under the heading, *Sentences I'd like to hear the end of*. There then appeared the words: "... *Called in MI5 because every time the chauffeur-driven Zils drew up at her front door, out of her back door into a chauffeur-driven Humber slipped...*"

The first car could only belong to the Russian Embassy. The chauffer driven Humber could only be for a politician. But which one? Perhaps Profumo was not the only one believed to have been giving away state secrets? It was known that Prince Philip was often seen in a Humber car.

At the same time the prime minister Harold Macmillan carried out what would later be called *The Night of the Long Knives*. This was when he either removed or reshuffled a third of his cabinet. Macmillan told the press that getting rid of some of the older staff and replacing them with younger, more energetic men, would help to win the next general election (due to take place by 1964). Among those who were removed was Selwyn Lloyd, who, although married, liked to entertain young servicemen of all nationalities. This was known by press and politicians alike but kept from the public. Profumo was safe. He was even being tipped to take over Macmillan before the next election. The last thing the opposition wanted was to face an English Kennedy.

What is interesting about the *Queens Magazine* rumour and the cabinet reshuffle is the timing. No one had yet spoken to Christine, who by now had finished with both Profumo and Ivanov. Could it be that there were other politicians up to no good? Many in the press believed that the Conservative Party had been in power for too long. After thirteen years it seemed as though whatever they did was wrong. Their polices looked either stale or ridiculous. Their politicians seemed out of touch with the public. A whole generation that had only known a Tory government had grown tired of their actions and just wanted change. The only thing the Conservatives had going for them in sixty-two was that the Labour Party were devoid of any solutions and looked just as incompetent and inept when it came to running the country.

Profumo argued that stability was the way forward. While French President General De Gaulle was almost killed in an assassination attempt in retaliation for Algerian independence, England safely oversaw the independence of the Bahamas with nothing more serious than a touch of sunburn. The rest of the year looked pretty good; especially with President Kennedy still proclaiming that America was going to put a man on the Sea of Tranquillity by the end of the decade. But the universe has a way of mooning in your face.

A year after the trial had finished, Adolf Eichmann was hanged. When the noose was put around his neck it is believed he said, "I hope that all of you will follow me". One wonders how many times his guards had stopped him from committing suicide in order to see justice served. Perhaps that spell in purgatory while waiting to be hanged was the greatest punishment he could have received. The decision had been correct and inevitable. He had shown no remorse.

As one trial ended that day, another had begun. Nelson Mandela had been arrested and charged with numerous offences including state sabotage, which in South Africa carried the death penalty. Mandela argued that his country belongs to the indigenous population, and indigenous culture should be the dominant force in this country rather than foreign influences. You could argue that those ideals were like the claims the white Englishman Tommy Robinson made outside the Old Bailey in 2019 in regard to the cover up of hundreds of white children being systematically raped by Muslims from India and Pakistan because the government did not want to be accused of racism. His was another trial where politics had taken precedence over justice. Although we can all agree that Robinson is not even half the man of Mandela. Tommy Robinson got nine months in prison; Mandela got twenty-seven years. When released he went on to become President of South Africa. Mandela died in 2013 at the age of ninety-five, leaving me to wonder that if half the politicians were just a quarter of the statesman he was, the whole world would be a better place.

There was other news in the summer of sixty-two. Marylin Monroe, the star every woman wanted to be, and every man wanted to bed, killed herself. The reason was never really made clear. The last time she had appeared in the news was wearing a nude dress singing happy birthday to the President in Madison Square Garden. Her looks were fading mostly due to the drink and drugs she was taking daily. There were rumours that she was sleeping not just with John Kennedy, but his brother Robert as well. There were also rumours that she had been "assisted" in helping to die because there was the worry that she might go on a live chat show smashed off her face and tell the truth. To stop this, somebody came to her home and started the process of an overdose. They may not have poured all the pills down her throat, but they helped her decide to do it.

The President lost some of his shine in the summer of sixty-two. The Bay of Pigs invasion had been a disaster. The communist Party always seemed to be two steps ahead in the space race, and the western world watched as a wall was built in Berlin. America looked weak. Another mistake and it could all be over. Most reporters knew that Kennedy had spent many different nights with many different women. If Marylin had confessed to having sex with JFK there could have been hundreds of women all over the world ready to ruin the good Catholic family man's reputation by saying "Me too."

~

They say we attract certain people because of who we are. Positive and negative individuals come into our life, and we must decide how much influence they will have. Sometimes it's a tough choice to make, and usually we only know if we've made the right decision when time has passed.

You could argue the sixties were not that great. Motorways carved out the countryside at the same time environmentally friendly trains and buses were disappearing. Ghastly tower blocks appearing in the skyline of every town as planners got rid of communities. The loss of these communities meant the loss of meaning for many people. Loneliness created the sense of an ending with every slouching step. Many of Ward's friends were getting older, getting married, and moving away.

In sixty-two Stephen Ward was going to turn fifty. This was not like turning fifty today. There were no gyms, no one jogged or ate protein bars, shorts were only allowed on the tennis court or the beach. People smoked from the age of sixteen; they smoked a lot, and they smoked everywhere. The living room, dinner table, pub, cinema. If you weren't smoking, you were near someone who was. And people drank. There were three times as many pubs as what there are now. Large factories had their own bars in the building. People went for a drink at lunchtime. Every high street had an off licence for you to buy alcohol while waiting for the pubs to open. People went to numerous social clubs, all of which had a bar.

This might not have been as bad as it sounds. Your local pub was just that, you went and socialised there on a Friday night or Sunday lunchtime. In fact, you could walk into any pub or club in your community and would know someone. The price of having a few years taken off your life by drinking and smoking was paired with the times you enjoyed the company of your friends while you could still remember their name instead of lying for hours in a hospital bed. For many they were willing to take the second option. Even the pot smoking Shakespeare all those years ago thought that three score years and ten, was the maximum time you should have on this mortal coil.

For Ward, who knew the average life expectancy for men in the nineteen-sixties was sixty-five, must have felt that the good times were behind him. One can feel young in their forties, but when you hit fifty there is a definite change in others perception of you. The number of attending funerals rises whilst the number of wedding invitations go down. Ward was a bachelor, divorced, no children, no family to visit, friends all quietly fading away. Perhaps it was time for him to settle down.

~

1962 would be the beginning of things. The same week The Beatles released *Love Me Do*, kick starting the swinging sixties; the film *Dr No* was released to British audiences. The book had been published in the fifties, but the film was definitely sixties. The reason being was Hitchcock's *North by Northwest* (which should have been a Bond film) was released in 1959. It had plenty of big action scenes, an attractive blonde, and a main character who was English (at least played by the Bristol born Cary Grant). As such the producers and director had to give *Dr No* a sixties feel to try and stop the comparisons to Hitchcock. It worked. It beat *To Kill a Mockingbird* and *The Trial* (both filmed in black and white) at the box office. The profits enabled the producers to decide to turn the first film into a franchise. It would seem people were more interested in scenes of Bond courting beautiful women than boring court scenes of women complaining about being held in bondage. Most men, including Stephen Ward, wanted to be like Bond. If you were helping your country, the rule of law didn't really apply. But as we headed into Christmas, the letter of the law was about to become extremely important.

Chapter 12.

The Winter of Discontent.

In 1962 Prince Charles was flown up to Gordonstoun School in Scotland by his father. Prince Philip had gone there when he was a child. The difference was that Philip was athletic and a risk taker. Charles, on the other hand, was far more reserved. It was rumoured that no one was happy with the situation apart from Philip, who hoped Gordonstoun would make his son more of a man.

There is a story of Ward when he was a boy at his public school, where he was made by the teachers to take the blame for something he had not done. Another child had been injured, and as no one came forward, the teachers decided to punish Ward knowing he was innocent. It's quite possible that this was to influence him later in life.

Perhaps the most serious account of how a childhood affects someone as an adult is that of Christine being sexually abused by her stepfather and some of his friends when she reached puberty. In the nineteen-fifties the men no doubt told her that she would never be believed if she went to the authorities.

Our childhood defines the person we become for the rest of our lives. We can all remember a moment when we have been a victim in our youth of harsh words, accused of something you didn't do, mental and physical bullying, or even worse. All of us keep those psychological and visible scars with us in one way or another, hoping the wounds would have healed by the time we become adults. But the past can sometimes strike when we least expect it. The feeling of not being loved as a child means you could end up falling in love with the wrong person as an adult. Being punished as a child can leave you unable to stand up to bullies as an adult. Many people are able move on, but some do not.

In the Autumn, Christine and Mandy travelled to New York to try and break into modelling/acting. They met and partied with some important people, but in 1962 it was hard to tell if that meant the President or the mafia. Chances are it was probably both. There was also another reason Christine wanted to get out of London. The situation between her and Lucky Gordon had become intolerable. He had beaten and raped her on more than one occasion. Like many victims of domestic abuse, she did not know how to escape from a bad relationship until she simply walked out of the door and decided not to go back. Unfortunately, also like many other victims of domestic abuse, the next person who promised to protect her turned out to be just as bad.

When she returned to London Christine formed a relationship with Johnny Edgecombe, an ex-merchant seaman from Antigua who was a drug dealer. She believed he was strong enough to stand up to Lucky Gordon. He and Gordon clashed violently on 27th October 1962, when Lucky found them in a dance hall. He confronted the couple, and Edgecombe slashed Gordon across the face with a knife. Such an incident should have resulted in Edgecombe going to prison, if anyone had called the police.

~

In May 1962 the playwright Joe Orton and his boyfriend Kenneth Halliwell were in court for defacing library books. Over the last few years, they had been doing things such as taking out a serious tome called *The Great Tudors* and replacing the portrait of Henry the Eight with a chimpanzee and Thomas Moore with the face of Terry Thomas. They also changed inner sleeves with their own account of the books plot. In *Clouds of Witness* by Dorothy L. Sayers, the unsuspecting reader would be enthralled to know that *This is the sort of book that should be read behind closed doors, having a good shit at the same time.*

For defacing a couple of library books both men were given five months in prison and ordered to pay £262. For Joe it was liberating.

The publicity gave him notoriety (every writer's dream), and even if he wasn't getting corn-holed every day, prison gave him time to meet other men with interesting stories. For Kenneth Halliwell incarceration became a slow descent into depression, murder and suicide.

When they were released that autumn Joe had a play broadcast on the radio. It would eventually lead to him being the toast of the West End. Having been a practicing homosexual for many years, his sex life now became extremely professional. Kenneth became a ghost in the relationship. A faceless memory as soon as he left the room. Orton tried to get Kenneth to show his pictures by paying for a gallery exhibition (perhaps even meeting Ward); but the work simply wasn't good enough.

Orton began to move with a different crowd, and away from Kenneth. Some people hate it when their friend become more popular than them. Kenneth took to drink and anti-depressants to try and keep the relationship going. When Brian Epstein wanted Orton to write the script for the Beatles film. Kenneth realised he and Orton were never going to be the next Lennon and McCartney. Kenneth killed Orton and then committed suicide using barbiturates. Orton was cremated at Golders Green to the song *A Day in the Life*. But let's go back to the news of the day.

In sixty-two, while Orton was in prison for putting photographs of cats on books, President Kennedy was shown photographs of missile bases in Cuba. Fidel Castro, just a few hundred miles from American soil, could soon have the capability of bringing Washington to its knees. Kennedy was told they were going to be used for Russian ballistic missiles, capable of carrying nuclear warheads.

Kennedy had a couple of options, most of them resulting in the start of World War Three. The generals seemed to want it. Kennedy didn't. He ordered the Navy and the air force to step up a blockade on all Russian ships heading towards Cuba but not to invade the island. The world watched and waited.

Castro felt that this was a direct aggression towards the Cuban people. Believing that Kennedy's mess in The Bay of Pigs fiasco showed his lack of leadership, decided to call the presidents bluff and told the Russians to continue to sail towards Cuba with ships loaded with military hardware. People began to work out how long it would take for missiles to reach the major cities in America and Russia. As the crises deepened, Secretary of State for War John Profumo knew that under the terms of Mutually Assured Destruction (MAD), England would also be a viable target.

Things became more heated on 27th October when an America U2 spy plane was shot down over Cuba and the pilot died in the crash. Kennedy was not sure if it was the Cubans or the Russians who had fired and so held back from retaliating. It was a wise move, as it later turned out to be Castro's decision to shoot. Castro, after not getting the response he wanted, sent Khrushchev a message demanding that if Cuba was attacked Russia should retaliate with all the nuclear weapons it had. Khrushchev must have thought Castro was a mad chihuahua trying to start a fight between two lions. The most powerful man in the world was also clever enough to know when he was getting played, so he held back all ships from sailing towards the island. Everyone waited, and waited, and waited.

After a few days Kennedy addressed the nation live on television. The stand-off was going to end. From now on any communist ship caught trying to get to Cuba would be met with extreme force. This was a bit of a shock for Khrushchev. The one thing the establishment wants, both left and right, is to remain established. Over the next few days, a secret deal was reached. Khrushchev would publicly remove all missiles from Cuba if Kennedy secretly removed his missiles based in Turkey. Both men agreed. Both claimed victory. Normal services had been resumed.

During this time of high anxiety life went on in London. At one of Ward's exclusive parties a politician stood in front of a group of friends giving his thoughts on the missile crisis. He was naked, and a young woman was on her knees giving him a blow job. It is not known if the audience were more interested in the oratory of the man or the oral actions of the woman. I am not an expert on public felatio, but to be able to speak to your fellow guests on such an important matter while maintaining an erection says something about the rigid standards of our politicians at the time.

The Cuban missile crisis was not the only skirmish between two superpowers that month. The race between Lucky Gordon and Johnny Edgecombe over Christine's body had become a land grab. Now in hiding from both men, Edgecombe went looking for her carrying a gun. Ironically it had been Christine who had bought it to protect herself from Lucky after he sent her the stitches that Edgecombe had given him and promised to give double the amount to Christine's face. Even though she had grown apart from Ward, she was still friends with Mandy, who was staying at Ward's flat in Wimpole Mews.

On 14th December 1962 Christine went to Ward's flat to try and figure out with Mandy where her life was going. The liaisons with Profumo and Ivanov had long gone; although we should remember an old Chinese proverb that says, "The faintest ink is better than the strongest memory". Which was relevant as Christine had kept a note from Profumo about missing a date with her. Although still young, Christine must have felt that she had missed her chance for the big time. And then Edgecombe arrived at the small mews demanding to be let in.

When refused he huffed and puffed, then fired several shots at the windows and front door. Mandy called Ward at work, who told her to call the police. He need not have worried. The average price of these former mews stables turned into flats is now a couple of million. The neighbours were probably more shocked to see a black man in their street than the gun in his hand.

Edgecombe escaped but was arrested a short time later and charged with attempted murder (why no charges against Mandy who was also in the address?). Somebody must have given his name to the police. Such a strange event in London at the time did not go unnoticed by the press. Christine Keeler was described as "a free-lance model" and Miss Marilyn Davies as "an actress". You also had a black man with a gun, rumours of drugs, and a doctor linked to the royal family.

Most reporters still worked and drank in Fleet Street. Inside *Ye Olde Cheshire Cheese* a few of the crusty old journalists realised they had already heard of some of the players in previous incarnations. Stephen Ward was publicly considered the4 doctor who was also an artist. In private, many journalists also knew of his private parties. Mandy was linked to the corrupt landlord Peter Rachman; but she was staying tight lipped. Unlike Christine, who told the press she was at Cliveden House in 1961 and had met Profumo and a Russian ambassador. Being as the rumour about an expensive British car pulling up as a Russian one drove away was published six months prior, it would seem reporters had already heard of what had been going on, they just needed an eyewitness.

The official line is that in the wake of the Edgecombe shooting, Christine began to talk indiscreetly about Ward, Profumo, and Ivanov. But it is far more likely that cheque book journalism got her to confirm (and embellish) what reporters already knew. Christine then gained an unlikely friend. John Lewis, the former Labour MP and a long-standing enemy of Ward, somehow met Christine by chance in a club near Baker Street. She poured her heart out. He passed the information to George Wigg, a ghastly unpopular Labour politician who was close to Harold Wilson. As leader of the opposition, Wilson knew the information was highly inflammatory, even enough to bring down Macmillan. He then made the decision not to bring it up in parliament. He wanted Macmillan to set a date for a General Election before going after him in Westminster and so told everyone to say nothing. But sometimes things gain a momentum of their own.

Chapter 13.

The mirror crack'd.

Before 1963 reporters knew about the secret lives of the establishment…and kept them secret. Quite often it was because the only media outlet they had available were newspapers, and most were owned by press barons who were members of the same clubs as the men they were going to expose. Another reason might have been because in the sixties if the police wanted to fit you up for a crime, they could, and they would. And if a judge wanted to find you guilty, they could, and they would. Staying silent meant staying alive.

Ward and Mariella Novotny continued organising sex parties for exclusive clients. By now journalists would have heard the rumour of her sleeping with JFK; but there was no chance of the press ever making it public. There was never any mention that Ivanov went to these orgies; no doubt he had been warned that there could be someone hiding behind a two-way mirror taking pictures of his person. This would have led to blackmail, and worse, the Communist Party taking personally. Getting sent home and to a Gulag was not worth it. It is believed Profumo had been warned by the Secret Service months ago about Ward's parties, and that was why he had written the "Darling" note cancelling his date and effectively ending the relationship with Christine. But that doesn't mean he stopped seeing Ward.

By Christmas the public felt it had gone past the peak of Cold War paranoia. The Conservative Party must have also felt they had weathered the storm. Believing he had a father/son relationship with Kennedy, and was still on talking terms with Khrushchev, Harold Macmillan must have thought he had a good chance of winning the next election and then retiring to a nice little cottage in the country after choosing the right successor. But circumstances beyond his control were gaining a momentum of their own.

~

MI6 agent Kim Philby, who was a friend of Ward's, had vanished while in Beirut in early January after rumours that another spy scandal was breaking. The government realised too late he was on a Soviet ship bound for Odessa. It then became clear he had been a communist spy for many years. The government decided not to go public with the information for fear of causing more embarrassment to themselves. Later, more rumours abounded with the story that MI6 had let Philby escape to Moscow rather than arrest him and face a trial which would have named many people within the establishment.

A few days later Yevgeny Ivanov was suddenly recalled back to Russia. Ironically, that Winter in London was reminiscent of Moscow, with snow covering the country for many months. Even in April there was still frost on the ground. For those that could reach the local cinema in the freezing cold the big film was Cliff Richard in *Summer Holiday*. The Beatles topped the charts with *From Me to You*.

In politics, Labour leader Harold Wilson was planning how to win the next election. Wilson was a middle-class northerner, which equated to being working class in parts of the south, and highly cultured by anyone from Leeds. He had got to the top through hard work and talent. He had won scholarships to grammar school and then university. After the war he battled through the political ranks to become Shadow Foreign Secretary. This meant he would have had numerous talks with Profumo over the independence of former colonial countries and their military bases.

Having been passed on information about the scandal from some of his Labour comrades at the start of January he must have wondered if the Russian Naval Attaché had left in such a hurry because someone in the Labour party had warned him. It may have also confirmed those rumours about Profumo/Ivanov and Christine Keeler were true.

Many in the Labour Party it felt one more scandal could bring the government down. But Wilson was clever enough to know that the election was winnable as along as Macmillan stayed in charge until the last possible moment. When they went to the polling booths people needed to remember that it was under Mac's watch that all this mess happened, and not a new leader filled with promises. As such Wilson didn't want to ask questions in parliament straight away. There was also the risk of having no proof. To besmirch England's answer to JFK may have a negative effect on voters, and even though those same voters liked a good scandal, Wilson couldn't afford to be wrong.

~

In March a trial began concerning the Duke and Duchess of Argyle. Married in 1951, they had regularly attended Ward's exclusive swinging parties in Mayfair. But over the years the duke had become addicted to painkillers and strong alcohol, softening his libido somewhat. The Duchess was made of sterner stuff and took on allcomers with her head held high. When the Duke decided to divorce the Duchess for infidelity, he claimed that at these parties she had slept with numerous men, including members of the Royal family and two government ministers. Most damming was a photograph of the duchess, naked except for her pearls, giving a blow job to someone who could not be identified as the image was cropped at the neck. It had been taken with a brand-new instamatic camera, of which there were only a few in the country at the time. The man had pointed the camera at a mirror, capturing the Duchess on her knees, and was kind enough to give her the picture for posterity. If anymore were taken, we do not know.

Lord Alfred Denning was tasked to try and identify the headless man. It was rumoured that politician Duncan Sandys (Minister of Defence) was the perpetrator. Another suspect was the actor Douglas Fairbanks Jnr (who also had a threesome with Christine and Mandy). The Duchess kept her mouth firmly closed when asked to name the braggard. The Duchess of Argyle then retaliated by accusing her husband of having an affair with her stepmother. All this was gripping stuff for the press, and they sold thousands more newspapers than usual.

The photograph was not enough to complete the divorce. A man had to be produced who would admit to sleeping with the duke's wife. The duke cited a long list of men, many of whom he knew (and so did she) to be homosexual. If they were forced to give evidence, they ran a strong chance of being asked about their sexuality and being outed in a public court. Rather than ruin the lives of her friends, the Duchess changed her plea and admitted that she had been unfaithful to her husband. The divorce was granted in the duke's favour. In closing, the judge described her as "completely immoral". His view of his good old friend the duke remained private.

The real winner in all this was the press. They had unlocked the bedroom door of the establishment and seen them caught with their trousers down. People wanted to know what the rich and powerful really got up to in the mansions of this green and pleasant land; and it turned out they were constantly rutting like drunken farmyard pigs. The duke, although a bit of a shit, got away from being vilified by the press because he was a man who had gone to the right schools and belonged to the right clubs. The old boy's network was not going to let one of their own chaps down (especially if he knew their secrets as well). It was clear to many that justice protected the few.

If Stephen Ward had been reading about the trial, he must have wondered if his name would ever pop up. He had been to the same parties, and it would have been easy for both the Duke and Duchess to call him to give evidence. It is quite possible that he was the naked headless man in the photograph, although it would be more likely that he was the one who took the picture.

By now Ward had problems of his own. In the last few weeks, the police had been asking a lot of questions about him and had even started watching his home and place of work. Since the shooting he had moved around the corner from Baker Street to another flat in

Bryanston Mews. With the headless felatio trial seemingly spent, Ward hoped things would get back to normal. But just when he thought he was out, the establishment pulled him back in.

The trial of Johnny Edgecombe for attempted murder had also begun. The star witness, a Miss Christine Keeler, had for some reason decided to go on holiday at this crucial time rather than give evidence. Newspapers, now aware of the Profumo/Ivanov scandal but unable to publish it, were offering thousands of pounds to find her. The Daily Express put a picture of her on the front page (next to a seemingly unrelated article about Profumo) with the headline *MISSING*.

Christine eventually came back to see Edgecombe convicted on the lesser offence of possession of a firearm and sentenced to seven years in prison. She then got back with Lucky Gordon, who went back to hitting her again.

In April she was at a friend's home when she was attacked by a man at the party. She told police it had been Gordon. He was arrested. A black man wasn't going to get much sympathy from the Metropolitan police in 1963, especially after being accused of assaulting a white woman. He told them there were witnesses who would prove he was innocent, and elected for trial, which would start in June. Ward must have thought it would soon all be over. But sometime things gain a momentum of their own.

And what of Ward in these last few months? The Argyle divorce trial had stopped most of his regular parties. His two proteges had not transformed into the famous stars he wanted them to be. Ironically, they would later find out what it was like to be infamous. And by this time, he was fully aware that Christine had spoken to the press. Ivanov had disappeared back to Russia. The Communist Party could easily say that they had got secrets from him, and in so doing the Secret Service would be looking at Ward as a possible Communist spy. At least he could look back at the last few years with the belief that he had behaved like an English gentleman.

But the past is never really the past. Some things never really go away. A meeting that happened one weekend two years ago now gained a significance far beyond what Ward thought it was. Someone was going to become a political sacrifice. Someone needed to be punished. Someone needed to be silenced for an extremely long time.

When we think of the past and the mistakes we made, quite often they relate to the things that we never did or the words we never said. But there are other mistakes that haunt us. The things we did say and actions we now regret. Those moments you cannot change or forget. Ward had spent his youth wasting time on pleasure. His religious parents faded away the moment he left for America. His war was fought in India, where he never faced the enemy. His wife divorced him because he saw nothing wrong in sleeping with other women. At the height of the Cold War, he was openly agreeing with some of the Communist policies. He believed in free thinking, free love, and freedom of speech. But in the end, everything has a price.

Chapter 14.

Cunnilingus and psychiatry brought us to this.

In late 1962 government worker John Vassall was arrested at his flat in Dolphin Square. It transpired he had been handing over state secrets since 1954, after Soviet spies had taken pictures of him in compromising positions with various men. He pleaded guilty at the start of his trial on 22nd October (the same day President Kennedy learnt about the Russian missile bases in Cuba) and was given 18 years in prison. He served ten. When he was released, he promptly collected his safety deposit box from a bank vault in Baker Street and bought a house in St. Johns wood. There were other rumours circulating at the time of his arrest. One of them was that the Russians exposed Vassall themselves because they believed MI5 were getting close to another spy higher up in the establishment.

Rather than go after the truth, the government went after the people trying to find it. Two well respected journalists, Brendan Mulholland and Reg Foster, were summoned to parliament to give evidence in relation to the Vassall enquiry. It felt a bit like a show trial. The government were asking a lot of questions apart from the obvious one: How did one man manage to blatantly steal secrets since 1954 and not get caught?

The politicians demanded to know where the two journalists had got their information from. They knew that John Vassall was a promiscuous homosexual who attended certain parties. Did they know who else attended, and who told the reporters. The government wanted a name. The two journalists realised they were not being accused of libel; they had not written anything that could be considered a blatant lie, as such they could not be sued. They believed there was there no need to disclose where they got their information from as it would breach the element of confidentiality that many journalists relied on.

The government changed tact, and the reporters were then accused of being in contempt of court (government enquiries are held under judicial regulations). This was a blatant breach of Judicial procedure, but the government went ahead anyway and found a judge willing to agree.

In January 1963 Mulholland was jailed for six months and Foster got three months for refusing to name the source who had given them details on Vassall.

The press in Fleet Street was at first shocked, and then angry. For over a century journalist had looked away when the establishment carried out their sexual, financial, and quite often illegal acts. The male reporters smiled when stories came in about young women and old politicians caught with their trousers down, knowing the story would never be published. But now the gloves were off. The press would make sure the next scandal would cause a knockout blow for the government.

The story of Christine Keeler and an attempted shooting quickly became one about Profumo and Ivanov. They kept Christine in the headlines when the original story should have faded away. What the press didn't realise was that they were also bringing Ward into the court of public opinion until he too became a person of interest. With Ivanov in another country and Profumo hiding in his country estate, Ward rose to the top of hit list. One night his home was burgled and some photographs were taken. He reported it to the local police station in Marylebone Road just off Baker Street. Among the pictures stolen were some he had taken in Cliveden in 1961, showing Christine and Profumo together. If he had other photographs somewhere, Ward kept quiet about them. The strange thing was that Ward believed the police were watching his flat at the time.

This one was in Bryanston Mews. It allegedly had a hole in the wall and on the other side was a mirror, so that Ward could take pictures of what was happening in the bedroom. The mirror bit was true, as the flat had been owned by Peter Rachman who ran a string of brothels that had now been taken over by Michael de Freitas.

~

If the Profumo scandal had simply been about sex, it would not have had such an overwhelming impact. It might have even been kept out of the news. Harold Macmillan thought this at the outset. "*I was forced to spend a great deal of today over a silly scrape; women this time, thank God, not boys*," he wrote in his diary on 15th March 1963. What made the "scrape" more serious, Macmillan believed, was that the Soviet naval attaché had been involved with Christine too. Again, this would not be so bad if the media had not decided to drag up an incident from two years ago to get back at the Tories. Ironically, there was another scandal before this, but it just wasn't sexy enough.

Kim Philby had worked as a government official for many years. He also worked for the Communists. During this busy period, he also had many affairs (women this time, not boys). His name was linked to other spies such as Guy Burgess, and later, Anthony Blunt. There was a rumour as far back as 1956 that he was a spy, but Harold Macmillan had stopped any investigation and declared Philby was an officer and a gentleman. When he defected in January the press had stayed quiet. Now they were beginning to ask questions, such as "Did the government let Philby escape to Moscow in order to avoid damaging questions?"

Macmillan now found himself reading again about a man whose name seemed to be cropping up in every scandal: Stephen Ward. Ward was still close to numerous members of government (including Winston Churchill), members of the Royal family, and Russian ambassadors. Macmillan must have thought it was all a bit too James Bond for it to be real. Unfortunately, there were also lurid stories about high up members of the establishment being involved in sexual high jinks at parties organised by Ward. No doubt Macmillan expected the whole ghastly business to go away.

It was on the 14[th of] March the press printed the missing Christine Keeler on the front page, and the politician John Profumo in a different article next to her. On the 21[st of] March, the satirical magazine *Private Eye* published a more prosaic version of Christine's rise to fame. To protect their innocence (and libel reasons) the names of certain people had been changed to "Mr James Montesi", "Miss Gaye Funloving", "Dr Spook" and "Vladimir Bolokhov". There was only one politician in government with an Italian name, Christine was staying at Dr Ward's flat at the time of the shooting, and it didn't take long to get from Ivanov to Bolokhov. The magazine was sold out by lunchtime that day.

The evening newspapers then reported on the magazines story without breaching libel laws themselves. It's a trick now used all the time by the mainstream media. Create a fake story linked to a real event, then put it on the news as a real story about the fake story.

Under parliamentary privilege, the Home Secretary Henry Booke was asked to deny any rumours between a politician, Miss Christine Keeler, and the Edgecombe shooting. It was an interesting move by the Labour Party. Asking a question that could only be answered by asking another question. Profumo and Ivanov were not mentioned, leaving Brooke unable to answer the question.

On 23rd March the press reported that Brooke had failed to answer an important question, but did not tell the public what the question was. This led to more speculation in the papers. At lunchtime Profumo stood up in Parliament and said that he acknowledged a friendship with Miss Christine Keeler and Dr Stephen Ward, the former of whom he had last seen in December 1961 purely on a friendly basis. He had met a "Mr Ivanov" twice, also in 1961. Profumo then stated: "There was no impropriety whatsoever in my acquaintanceship with Miss Keeler" and added: "I shall not hesitate to issue writs for libel and slander if scandalous allegations are made or repeated outside the House."

That afternoon, Profumo was photographed at Sandown Park Racecourse in the company of the Queen Mother. Ironically, among the guests that day in Westminster was Jeremy Thorpe, who would later face trial for conspiracy to murder his former boyfriend in 1979 and be acquitted after a judge called the victim "a fraud, a sponger, a whiner, and a parasite".

The people reading the newspapers the next day must have wondered what the fuck was going on. What had started out as a question over a domestic incident now appeared to involve international espionage. With the press keeping Christina close to their chest, the name of Stephen Ward kept cropping up. Ward went to Secret Service Headquarters and tried to see Mr Woods, the man he had met on previous occasions, only to be told that no one of that name existed. He then went to Westminster and was told to stand by Profumo in public and deny any impropriety.

On the 27th of March, the Home Secretary, Sir Henry Brooke, along with the head of MI5, and the commissioner of the metropolitan police, held an urgent meeting. It was here the fateful decision was made to go after Ward. But why? Surely Christine was the one who knew what went on between her, Profumo and Ivanov? No, for some reason Ward was the real danger. Four days after Profumo declaring he had done nothing wrong, the government, the Secret Service, and the head of the largest police force in the country, decided that Dr Stephen Ward was guilty, but of what?

The first issue was that he had been speaking to (working for?) the Secret Service prior to Cliveden. He had also been in contact with them throughout 1962. If it became known that they knew about Profumo and Ivanov two years ago and did nothing, it would be a catastrophe.

The next issue was that Ward was an osteopath who had treated many famous people, including a former prime minister, members of royalty, and many other politicians. Imagine having to ask them if any security breaches had taken place while they lay naked on a massage table.

And then you had the final issue. Everyone was aware Ward had been involved in sex parties since the 1950's. Politicians, celebrities, criminals, the rich and powerful, all enjoying each other's company while naked. If Ward had any photographic evidence, it could be very damaging. It would be better if he was to just disappear altogether.

~

But let's go back a bit to that question asked during a seemingly long and boring parliamentary debate. George Wigg, an inadequate politician and apparently an awful man, stood up on the Labour benches and asked the Home Secretary Baron Brooke if there was any truth in the rumours between "a minister and a miss Christine Keeler and a Mr Edgecombe currently on trial for attempted murder." Brooke knew the truth but said he had no idea. Labour MP Barbara Castle, a good politician and apparently a very good person, then asked if any attempt to pervert the course of justice (by a politician) had taken place. Although no names had been mentioned, especially any Russian ones, it was Profumo who mentioned Ivanov and Ward when he spoke the next day?

   This must have been cleared by the government and the Secret Service. The establishment must have told Profumo to deny any sexual relationship with Christine, and knowing the press were aware of Ivanov, to also deny meeting him on more than one occasion. After the Vassall case the government knew the press wanted blood. Who better than a doctor involved in sordid sex parties.

   Stephen Ward had spent the last few years living a dream life. He had met film stars, partied with members of the royal family, and carried out every sexual indulgence he could think of. He had a flat in London, a cottage in the country, a sports car, a string of young girlfriends, constant access to drink and drugs, and enough money to enjoy the finer things in life. Everything in the garden had been rather lovely, until now.

   If paranoia is one of the symptoms of anxiety and depression, Ward must have felt slightly uneasy in the Spring of sixty-three. You may think the fact that he killed himself and was therefore not of sound mind is a clue, but there were no signs of depression in those last few years. There is a belief today that some personality disorders lessen with age, but I don't know if the research is based on women or men who had been treated when they were young and are now able to manage their condition.

The Profumo scandal broke just as Ward was going through a possible crisis. Some middle-aged men today like to dress in the same type of clothes they wore as a teenager, secretly go online looking for one-night stands, get tribal tattoos and a hat to wear at a festival. Ward had reached a point where his old friends were leaving him, and his new friends were just using him.

And when does a mid-life crisis begin? In 1960 you could say that you got it in your mid-thirties; Shakespeare's three score years and ten still seemed relevant. But here was Ward, now in his fifties, essentially an old man, smoking pot and sleeping with women young enough to be his daughter. This desperate need to feel alive through drink and drugs was taking its toll, and unfortunately there is no chemical cure to a spiritual problem. Watching other people have sex will never satisfy the desire to be loved, and now the police were watching his every move.

I wonder if as a youth he walked with his father through St. Albans cathedral. Did he ever wonder if being a martyr was worth dying for? Even with all the fame and wealth that Stephen Ward had acquired over the years, the son of a village vicar would soon be God's loneliest man. For within a matter of weeks the highest court in the land would be getting ready to cast judgement on him.

Chapter 15.

The Old Bill and the Old Bailey.

It begins.
On 1st April 1963 the Metropolitan Police officially start to investigate the private affairs of Mr Stephen Ward. If the allegation was related to spying, the Secret Service would have overseen the operation, but they don't. We must assume this was a straightforward criminal investigation. But no one had accused Ward of anything criminal. We would be looking at the resources of at least six detectives, two detective sergeants, a detective Inspector, a detective chief Inspector, and a detective superintendent, all having to stop doing their normal duties to deal with Ward. There would also be a lot of other people on the side-lines helping to gather information. In today's money that would be about five hundred thousand pounds allocated from the police budget to investigate someone who hasn't yet been alleged of doing anything wrong. Let's say that again…At that time the police started to investigate the British citizen Dr Stephen Ward, he had not been accused of any crime. The authorisation to go after an innocent man could only have come from someone at the very top.

The start of every police investigation is that a victim or witness contacts the police to report a possible criminal offence, and enquiries are then made to either confirm or negate if the law had been broken. But not for Ward. Certain people in MI5 and the government decided that Ward should not be allowed to disclose anything to the public that may cause further embarrassment. What they didn't have was a crime to silence him with. They knew about his parties. The problem was that at these parties were some very influential people. They knew about his political views. Ward believed that women should have as much sexual freedom as men. He also thought communism had some good ideas. Again, there was a problem with this as many other influential people also believed in these ideas. He had never blackmailed anyone as far as they were aware, but there were rumours about him having a collection of photographs that could cause problems. If they could link Ward to something serious it would mean a prison sentence.

They started to maintain a 24-hour watch on Ward's home. They tapped his personal and business telephones. As he had not been alleged to have committed any crime at this stage and was not suspected of being a spy, again, authorisation must have come from the very top of government. The police started to stand outside his place of work and question his patients as they arrived and left. Why, no one was really sure, but soon the appointments slowed until all that was left were spaces in-between the lines on a faded appointment book. Ward tried to find out what was happening but got silence from both the police and Westminster.

For the next two months the police spoke to 147 people without telling them what they were looking for, just general questions about Ward. For many the experience of having a detective asking about their relationship with the man was enough for them enough to stay away from Ward for good even if he hadn't done anything bad. No one wanted the police to start prying into their own personal lives as well. The stories went back to the early fifties and before the Queen's Coronation. There were rumours of orgies in grand houses, whipping parties near Westminster, and an exclusive get together where the centrepiece in the dining table was a very large, very detailed, sculptured penis carved out of ice. There was also another party where someone at the very top of society wearing nothing but a mask and an apron and asking to be punished. Ward's friends knew that if any one of the parties they had attended reached the eyes and ears of the public it would be ruin. Best avoid dealing with the problem at all. And soon Ward noticed that the phone stopped ringing, and the requests stopped coming.

The portrait artist had always been a likeable libertine, the sort of gossipy storyteller that every stranger wanted to know at parties. The problem was that society had changed. These secret sexual liaisons everyone enjoyed as harmless fun in 1953 might not be regarded as such by the press in 1963, who now felt that the establishment needed be taken down a peg or two. Ward bringing a Communist over for drinks was amusing two years ago, but since the Cuban missile crisis the joke was flatter than yesterday's lemonade.

Among those interviewed by the police in relation to Ward was Christine Keeler. In fact, she was taken to a police station and "interviewed" no less than twenty-five times about him. What exactly she had to say on each occasion we do not know. There are no records kept of these meetings, and if there are, we are not allowed to see them. No doubt she confirmed her sexual relationship with Profumo, providing corroborative details of the interior of his London townhouse. But as for how we got from having sex with a politician to being pimped by Ward makes me wonder what threats may have been used by the police for her to finally crack.

Mandy Rice-Davies was arrested and remanded in Holloway Prison for using a provisional driving licence. Peter Rachman had got her one from Ireland because it was easier. Mandy should have got a full British driving licence within six months, but she had no idea she had to. For that heinous crime she was held in prison for eight days until she agreed to testify against Ward. Meanwhile, Profumo was awarded costs and £50 damages against an Italian magazine that had printed a story hinting that he might not have told the whole truth in parliament.

On 18th April 1963 Christine was attacked at the home of a friend by an unknown male. For some reason she accused Lucky Gordon, who was arrested and held on remand. Gordon was to later say that, just like Mandy, the police visited him in prison and ordered him to testify against Ward. He refused.

By now Ward realised he was being watched. What he didn't know was why, nor what the police were looking for. Whenever he tried to find out what was happening, he came up against a wall of silent bureaucracy.

On 7th May Ward met Harold Macmillan's private secretary, Timothy Bligh, to ask that the police inquiry into his affairs be halted. He added that he had been covering for Profumo, whose Commons statement was substantially false, to help the Conservative Party remain in power. He got no reply.

On 19th May Ward wrote to the Home Secretary Henry Brooke, with essentially the same request, only to be told that the Home Secretary had no power to interfere with a police inquiry. Of course, this was a blatant lie, as it was Brooke who had helped initiate the investigation into Ward.

Ward then wrote to the opposition leader Harold Wilson asking for help. Wilson showed the letter to Macmillan, who asked the Lord Chancellor to inquire into possible security breaches. Ward hoped that the Labour politician would at least make a stand for a man who was being shackled by the system. He was wrong. Labour were just as corrupt as everyone else. The reply came back that there was no one in government that could help him. Ward, the man who had served his country in war and in peace now found himself alone against the establishment. Even worse, it felt as if the whole of the Metropolitan police were investigating him for a crime he had not committed.

On 31st May at the start of the parliamentary Whitsun recess, Profumo and his wife flew to Venice for a short holiday. Reaching their hotel, they received a message asking Profumo to return as soon as possible. They arrived back in England to find that Macmillan was officially on holiday in Scotland. There appears to be a lot of secret meetings taking place even though everyone seems to be somewhere else.

On Tuesday 4th June, Profumo gave another speech to the House in which he (almost) said he had lied to Parliament. "To my very deep regret I have to admit that this was not true, and that I misled you and my colleagues and the House." He then resigned from the government. The resignation was announced on 5th June.

Newspapers published further sensational stories hinting at widespread immorality within Britain's governing class. Mandy Rice-Davies spoke about a naked masked man who acted as a waiter at sex parties; rumours suggested that he was a cabinet minister or possibly a member of the Royal Family. If the government thought everything would go away after a few days, they were wrong. Reporters had not forgotten how badly they had been treated over the Vassall case. Someone like Ward would be the ideal way to punish those in power.

Lucky Gordon's trial for the attack on Keeler began the same time Profumo's resignation was made public. Again, no matter what sort of person he was, every trial should be based on the evidence in relation to the crime committed. Gordon maintained that his innocence could be established by two witnesses, who, the police told the court, could not be found. The police said nothing as Christine gave evidence to say that she had been assaulted by Gordon.

On 7th June the jury found Gordon guilty of assault. He was sentenced to three years' imprisonment. At this point it is worth noting that the detectives sitting with Christine in court were the same ones who were investigating Ward.

The following morning, Saturday 8th June, Ward was visiting Bill Lang, a film maker friend in Watford, just a few miles from Borehamwood, when the police knocked on the door. He asked officers to speak to him a bit further down in Hempstead Road so as not to embarrass his friend. The detectives obliged. They listened and chatted for a while, then arrested Ward on suspicion of immorality offences.

Watford is about twelve miles away from Bryanston Mews, and at the time Ward was living alone, so how did the police know where he was? There is nothing to suggest that any new evidence had come to light in the last few hours. Ward could have been arrested weeks ago if the police had so wished but they waited until after Profumo had resigned (and so avoiding any questions in parliament).

Also of note, Ward was arrested just after midday. In 1963, to get bail you had to go in front of a judge or a magistrate, both of which only sat until midday on a Saturday. As the courts did not run on a Sunday, even with the best solicitor in the world, Ward was going to be held in police custody over the weekend until Monday.

On Sunday 9th June, free from Profumo's libel threats, the *News of the World* published "*The Confessions of Christine*". As well as lurid tales of lust with a politician and a spy, it was an account which helped to fashion the public image of Ward as a sexual purveyor and probable cohort of Soviet agents.

Profumo's "Darling" letter to Christine, the exhibit which had effectively showed Profumo to be a liar, was published in The Sunday Mirror (as they were willing to pay the most for it). Ward was unable to give his side of the story as he was in a cell helping the police with their enquiries. On the plus side The Beatles first album, *Please Please Me,* was number one in the charts.

~

We can question whether the English in 1963 were living in a police state, but for all intents and purposes the answer would be no, not quite. People were just more scared of the justice system. The law was upheld because if you were accused of breaking it, no matter how innocent you were, there was always a chance you could be found guilty. Imagine if you had been arrested for theft in 1963. There is no CCTV, no electronic devices to prove where you were, witnesses who could be forced to change their minds, and a copper was willing to swear on oath that they saw you committing a crime. Being booked into custody was all done by pen and paper. Any injuries and the police would say that you slipped. There was no twenty-four hours until you had to be charged or bailed. Some people were kept in custody for three days before they walked out of the station. Unless you had your own solicitor you were stuffed. Interviews were not recorded. You could spend hours with two detectives only to sign a blank piece of paper which would later be filled in with a full confession. Once in court the police would always be believed. Any member of the jury would certainly not want to upset them.

This is what Ward would have believed when he sat in an interview room with a pile of statements in front of him and the police saying he was a ponce. Although we should say we don't know what was said in these interviews, as nothing appeared to be written down, and no official record has ever been published. This is so bizarre that at the trial the judge even had to question why nothing was written down for what was a high-profile investigation.

There would have been at least two detectives in the room, with one of them taking notes. Perhaps it was because Ward was able to prove his innocence in answer to every question that nothing was produced as evidence. It didn't matter. Thirty-six hours after being arrested Ward was charged with Living off the Immoral Earnings of prostitutes and refused bail.

~

On Monday Ward was taken before a judge, who ordered that he be remanded in prison, in the belief his crimes were so foul that he deserved to be locked up before innocence or guilt had been proved. This seems utterly bizarre.

The press now realised something else was going on and turned their attention away from the government and towards the activities of Ward. While waiting for the trial to be set, Macmillan instructed Lord Denning to investigate and report on the growing rumours about politicians involved in sex parties. Because of the trial and Lord Denning's enquiry, the government were able to put a D-Notice on the press. This allowed them to see any articles before they were published and to block or release any stories. The ones showing Ward to be a cad were available to read. The ones showing him to being innocent were cancelled.

Ward's committal proceedings began a week later at Marylebone magistrates' court, where the Prosecution's evidence was fully reported in the press. To clarify, it was only the police who were allowed to tell their side of the story, and this was what was published in the newspapers. Ward was not given the opportunity to give his account about any of the accusations apart from pleading "Not Guilty" after every charge. The public would now be given time to read what the prosecution had to say before the trial had started. Some of those same members of the public would also be members of the jury a few weeks later.

The Ward case now sub judice, and the press were not allowed to give any further details until the trial was over. So, they pursued other stories. It was reported that Scotland Yard had begun an inquiry in parallel with Lord Denning's, looking into "homosexual practices as well as sexual laxity" among civil servants, military officers and MPs. The D-Notice was still in place, ordering newspapers not to publish anything that might be a breach of national security. What these reasons were, no one knew. Although there were always some editors who tried to bend the rules.

On 24th June the *Daily Mirror*, under the heading "Prince Philip and the Profumo Scandal" dismissed what it termed the "foul rumour" that the prince had been involved in certain sexual acts when he attended some of Ward's parties. Being as both Ward and the Prince had been members of The Thursday Club for over ten years, where debauchery was common, and women from Murrays Cabaret Club would often come over to work as "Hostesses", it was certainly true that they knew each other. The *Mirror* got around the D-Notice by reporting on how shocked they were about the story rather than the story itself. The government was beginning to lose control. They needed something to deflect attention away from the prince.

Less than a week later the government informed the press that Kim Philby had been a spy for many years and had defected to Moscow in January. Journalists began to look through their old reports. Philby had been working for British Intelligence since the start of the second world war. He had been accused by the press of being "The Third Man" in the Cambridge spy ring in 1955 but had been personally cleared by Harold Macmillan. To try and deflect any blame, Macmillan also claimed 1955 was the first time he had heard of Stephen Ward.

~

One hundred and forty-seven people. That's what it took to get Stephen Ward to court in 1963. That's not a hundred and forty-seven people who were victims of a crime he had been involved in. Nor were they all witnesses who were able to say they had seen Stephen Ward commit an offence. The police took a hundred and forty-seven statements to finally get eight charges from six victims. Ironically, the main evidence would come from the two women who had been friends with Ward before Cliveden and the Profumo affair.

The number of statements is important for another reason. It doesn't mean a jury would have to read all of them, it simply shows the level of time and resources the police were willing to take to have Stephen Ward arrested. The average murder case does not contain this many witness statements, but the police needed them to try and find anything they could charge Ward with. At least when it came to the trial it would be the first time the public would get to hear the whole story, wasn't it?

Part Four

I see all the birds are flown.

Chapter 16.

The Goddess of the eternal court of history.

The truth is we would probably find him guilty. For a start all the evidence pointed towards him committing the offence. The definition of murder was made out in black and white. When you looked at all the facts and listened to the witnesses you believed that he did it. The result should have come back that he had been found guilty beyond all reasonable doubt. But something happened that not even the judge could have foreseen: The jury. What changed the minds of the twelve jurors in that hot and sticky room was not cold hard facts but emotion. To ruin this poor man's life seemed incredibly harsh when it came to proving beyond all reasonable doubt that he did it. What if there was the slightest chance that he hadn't? The jury followed their heart, and the defendant was found not guilty. And so, thanks to Henry Fonda in *12 Angry Men,* one man was set free. But when you look at all the evidence, there seems little doubt that the son killed his father.

It's a great film, but criminal trials should not be decided on emotion. They must be judged within the definition of the law by the evidence alone. Of course, if that was the case, there would be no miscarriages of justice. A jury makes their decision based on what they have seen and heard; and if the evidence is flawed, witnesses not telling the whole truth, perhaps even corrupt police officers, then that is what a jury will use to decide a man's guilt or innocence. On 22nd July 1963, Ward entered court 1 of the Old Bailey hoping that the last thing the jury was going to base their decision on was their feelings.

The prosecution barrister was Mervyn Griffith-Jones; he of the Lady Chatterley's Lover farrago. If he didn't like what Mellor's had done with the lady in the woodshed, he was positively shocked with what Ward had done with the fallen women in the Wimpole Mews.

The defence barrister for Ward was Queens Counsel (QC) James Burge. He would later become the inspiration for John Mortimer's fictional barrister Horace Rumpole in his *Rumpole of the Bailey* stories. Burge was good, but he had a major flaw. He was under the misconception that British justice was fair and impartial.

Presiding over preceding's was the judge Sir Archie Pellow Marshall. The small man rotund man with features like a pickled onion was born in 1899. His ideals were a little less Victorian and rather more Spanish Inquisition, especially when it came to sex. As a political liberal, he hated real liberals like Ward. He had been chosen to get what the establishment wanted – Ward silenced. He watched with a sneer on his face as the defendant came into the court and was placed in the dock.

The charges were as follows:

Count 1: Living off the immoral earnings of Christine Keeler between the dates of June 1961 and February 1962 whilst she was living at Wimpole Mews.

Count 2: Living off the immoral earnings of Mandy Rice-Davies between October 1962 (when Ward took her in after she tried to commit suicide) *and December 1962, while she was living at Wimpole Mews.* (It was also during this time that Ward let her family stay in the address to help Mandy recover.)

Count 3: Living off the immoral earnings of Ronna Ricardo and Vicki Barrett between January and June 1963. (What is interesting is that by then Ward had moved to the flat in Bryanston Mews, which had been owned by Peter Rachman and no doubt used as one of his exclusive brothels over the years. It is quite possible that Ronna and Vicki had used the address before.)

Count 4: To procure a girl under twenty-one to have unlawful sexual intercourse. The prosecution put it to the jury that Sally Norie (the young lady who was also at Cliveden that weekend in 1961) had been pressured into having sex with Ward.

Count 5: To procure a girl under twenty-one to have unlawful sexual intercourse. This victim was a shop assistant who had sex with Ward after allegedly being lured away by Christine.

The indictments were all so weak they should never have been cause for any investigation, or even an arrest, and should never have reached a charging decision. But there is a slight conflict. Any member of the jury would have taken one look at Ward and realised something was wrong for one simple reason: he was rich. Not wealthy; but he had his own business, no doubt made money from his art and had wealthy friends. He did not need to be a pimp. Strangely, he had asked both Christine and Mandy for money. The reason, using the telephone in 1963 was expensive. Ward didn't like using them and certainly didn't like paying the bill. He had asked both women for money the same way a father tries to get money out of his children to try and get them to curb their usage. It was a couple of pounds each. For the prosecution, it was a million-dollar charge.

But Ward still found himself in the dock and still had to go through a trial. Like Macbeth, he was facing the prospect of being judged tomorrow, tomorrow, and tomorrow, creeping on at a petty pace from day to day, as the newspapers bubbled around the Old Bailey casting a spell on readers and jurors alike.

In truth the trial had been rushed through the criminal justice system at breakneck speed. The police had spent four months building a case. Ward and his defence team had been given two weeks to get trial ready. He knew most of the charges were rubbish, the difficulty would be getting the jury to see that they were. In the opening words of Griffith-Jones to the twelve good men at the trial, Mr Ward was a "thoroughly filthy fellow". This was not evidence; this was not what any one of the victims or witnesses had called him; this was just something that the barrister thought the defendant was. How's that for a fair trial.

~

To be a juror at crown court you merely had to not have a criminal conviction and be able to read and write. A person's mental capacity for understanding what was going on did not seem to be a worry. Once they had been sworn in, they would take their seat and listen to the opening salvos from the two barristers. The thrust of the prosecution's case related to Christine and Mandy being prostitutes and giving Ward money from their payments for sex. With this money he would then use it to pleasure himself with other young women. It should be noted that Ward's approximate income at the time from his medical practice and his portraits was around £5,500 a year; that is well over a hundred thousand pounds in today's money.

The right honourable Mervyn Griffith-Jones also pointed out that Ward was representing "the very depths of lechery and depravity", but never bothered telling the jury how much extra money Ward had earned from his lickerish lasciviousness. Poor Ward must have been working Christine and Mandy day and night in order to live the life he was accustomed to. But the financial situation of Dr Stephen Ward was never fully explained to the jury. Griffith-Jones was told to keep it simple and go for the jury's heart rather than their head. The other offences seemed more about Ward being a man of bad character than a real criminal.

The defence barrister Burge was rather hoping that the jury would see through the prosecutions shallow name calling and rely on the facts. It should also be noted that Burge, like many other people working in the justice system, knew that the conviction of Lucky Gordon assaulting Christine was going to be reviewed in a matter of days. It had been rumoured there was a recording of Christine saying that she had lied about being assaulted by him and the two witnesses who the police had been unable to trace had now come forward and were willing to state on oath that Christine had lied while on oath. If the appeal court found in favour of Lucky, the conviction would be quashed, and he would be released. Christine would then face the possibility of being arrested for perjury, and more importantly, it would throw out three of the main indictments against Ward as her evidence would be deemed as deeply flawed.

Burge also knew the prosecution had to prove beyond all reasonable doubt that Ward had committed the offences he had been accused of. For those with any legal knowledge this was probably the weakest case that had ever come to the Old Bailey. As long as the justice system was honest and fair, both Burge and Ward must have felt that the real trial would be the court of public opinion. If the jury were swayed by seedy stories in the press, they might find Ward guilty by association.

~

The media storm which surrounded this case had certain comparisons with the O. J. Simpson trial thirty years later. The celebrity sport and film star had been accused of murder after his ex-wife and a waiter who was returning her reading glasses had been found dead on the doorstep of her house. Simpsons blood was found at the scene, along with the shoeprints that belonged to a specific type of shoe he wore, and his glove found nearby. Add to that, there were clothes found inside his address which had the victims' blood on them, his total lack of alibi for the time they were murdered, his strange behaviour when told about his wife's death, and cuts on his hand which were deep enough to have caused him to bleed, all pointed to his guilt.

The media went into overdrive by turning it into a societal, racial, and political issue. The racist white detective Mark Fuhrman was no match for the racist black lawyer Johnny Cochran, the man in charge of defending Simpson. Stories of drugs and sex parties seemed to gain more headlines than the deaths themselves. During the trial Cochran and the defence team made it all about skin colour to save Simpson. Thirty years before this the prosecution team against Ward made the trial all about the skin trade to try and sink him.

Both trials asked the question: how do we assign innocence and guilt when our opinions have been influenced by the media? In the

1960's you had newspapers, radio, and television, all competing for the consumers attention. By the time of the Simpson trial in the early nineties the media had grown a hundred times in size, and apart from the press, they could give live feeds twenty-four hours a day. The owners and shareholders were also seeking to get rich from the news and found the more sensational the story the more money they made.

This was made clear when the mostly black jury in the Simpson trial listened to the evidence of how Simpson used to beat his white wife and were told it was because she had white privilege. They sat as the trial went on, and on, and on, creeping at a petty pace from day to day as the defence team questioned every aspect of the investigation. It was clear that they were being well paid by Simpson, while the prosecution were relying on justice. This went on for nearly a year even though Simpson refused to give evidence. The jury left the court, went back to their room, and within 48 hours reached a verdict of not guilty.

Most white people could not believe it. One detective had been called a racist; but he could not have planted all the evidence, and surely Simpson would want to stand in the dock and declare he was innocent, wouldn't he? But his lawyer had constantly told the jury that the police were systematically racist and so what was the point? A lot of black people said that they were glad Simpson had got away with murder. After years of black men going to prison for crimes they hadn't done, here was a guilty black man walking free.

I don't know if the jury *really believed* he was innocent or just thought like *12 Angry Men* there was not enough to prove his guilt. The prosecution believed that letting a jury made up of far more black people than what was representative of the population wasn't a problem as long as there were more women than men. The prosecution believed the evidence of Simpson's physical abuse against his ex-wife would be enough to punch through a guilty verdict. They were wrong. The defence kept it simple; this was all about black and white.

In England a jury is picked anonymously. The first time the barristers see them was when they walked into court. This is in so they cannot be threatened or bribed to change the outcome of any trial. But you couldn't stop them from being influenced by outside sources prior to the trial starting. Burge and his defence team believed the way Ward would win was to discredit the victims and witnesses. They were wrong. The prosecution were also planning to discredit them as well. They wanted ward to implicate himself morally and get the jury to think it's the same as being guilty.

If Ward had just been sleeping with prostitutes it would have been seen as embarrassing, but not the crime of the century. By labelling him as a pimp, even his medical abilities as a skilled osteopath were now somehow seen as sordid. Ward, who always dressed in a smart suit and glasses, was condemned by the rich newspapers for being louche, disliked by the middle-class papers because of his loose sexual mores, and hated by the working-class papers because of his links with the establishment. And all this before any evidence had been heard.

Chapter 17.

Christine in the box.

Perhaps the most important part of any trial is that the accused has committed a crime in the literal sense.

Under the Sexual offences act of 1956, the definition for Living off Immoral earnings is in two parts:

(1) It is an offence for a man knowingly to live wholly or in part on the earnings of prostitution.

(2) For the purposes of this section a man who lives with or is habitually in the company of a prostitute, or who exercises control, direction or influence over a prostitute's movements in a way which shows he is aiding, abetting or compelling her prostitution with others, shall be presumed to be knowingly living on the earnings of prostitution, unless he proves the contrary.

So, for Ward to be guilty he must have known Christine and Mandy were prostitutes, and he must have been taking money from them on a regular basis. Ward would also be considered to be living on the earnings prostitutes unless he was able to prove otherwise, such as having a regular job, wage slips, a bank account. But within the definition there are also other aspects. The women involved would have to be prostitutes. If they earned a wage or were given money by a partner, then the definition is flawed. To live off another's earnings is more than just sharing the spoils or taking a cut, it suggests that the only thing keeping Ward in his life of luxury was a stable of harlots he ran from his mews flat.

First up in the witness box was Christine Keeler. The prosecution would first have to prove she was a prostitute. The definition of a prostitute at that time was someone who engages in arbitrary sex for money. Arbitrary means they are not particular with whom they have sex with as long as they paid for it. There is no proof of Christine offering herself to everyone for money. But let's be generous and include the term of 'Escort' into the mix. An escort may be more particular, they may even hire themselves out not purely for sexual purposes; but they are still essentially selling themselves. This could also include the girls at Murray's Cabaret Club who would sit with gentlemen and spend time with them. If a woman had sex with someone after they had been bought a nice meal, or the person had given them money after the act to get a taxi or a new dress, was that prostitution? And this was probably the level that Christine Keeler ever reached in the annals of soliciting; she was at best a Tinder date.

Importantly, the intimate relations that Christine had with Profumo and Ivanov were not part of the offence. Neither man had given her money prior to sex taking place, if they had, Christine never put it in a statement. But as they happened in the time the offences Ward had been charged with; you would think that they would be important to the case. Perhaps she only ever had sex with them on her days off? Ivanov had already gone back to Mother Russia by the time the story broke, and Profumo had gone back to his wife in Surrey by the time the trial started. So, who are all these other men she slept with (for money) that are integral to secure a conviction? It would seem that no one really cared, certainly not the police. The only person who did admit to sleeping with Christina was Noel Howard-Jones (nothing to do with *New Song*) who gave evidence as a character witness for Ward, telling the jury he and Christina were in a relationship at the time.

The prosecution painted Christina as a harlot, yet they did not ask when she became a prostitute, how many men she had slept with, and how much she had earned while on the game. They left it to the jury to make their own mind up. All Griffith-Jones had to do was prove Christina had given Ward some money (irrespective of how much) and then go back to the last person who had given her cash after she had slept with them. Christina could have said that she never asked for any money beforehand and so negate the idea of being a prostitute, but the judge wouldn't let her speak. Again, it didn't matter. If the question from Griffith-Jones was 'Did you sleep with this man?' and the answer was 'yes', you simply asked another question along the lines of 'Did he ever give you money?' Who cares when the money was handed over or the reason behind it. The jury were reminded that sex and money was involved in the deal. The more difficult part was that they also had to believe that Stephen Ward was living off her immoral earnings.

~

First, there is no record of how much Christine was earning during the last two years; whether from selling her body or just having a job. Murrays was very much a cash only affair and there was nothing strange in a man inviting her out for a few drinks and a meal. She admitted some men gave her money, but it was to buy things with rather than as a transaction. She also admitted that she had only slept with a couple of men between 1961 and 1963. On that note you could also say that Christine wasn't very good at her job. If she had only slept with five or six men over two years, she clearly wasn't earning enough to keep herself in Mars Bars let alone giving her landlord Stephen Ward enough to live on. At the very most she was a good time girl out for a bit of fun, but she was never a prostitute.

Let's also consider that Stephan Ward had to be *living* off Christine Keeler's immoral earnings. This means more than Christine giving him money for the phone bill or going halves on a takeaway, he had to be profiting so much from her (and other prostitutes) that he could not financially survive without them. For the offence to be made out Christine would have to be sleeping with about six men a day. Under its own definition, this indictment should not have reached court. But the prosecution had not spent thousands of pounds getting Ward into the Old Bailey to let him walk straight back out. They wanted their pound of flesh.

Christine's evidence was neither good nor bad. She had the threat of perjury from the Gordon trial hanging over her, which the police knew but kept it secret from the jury. She answered the questions quietly and often with the comment that she wasn't sure. This left the jurors looking at the barristers for direction, and again it was the prosecution that won the battle. The judge never stepped in and stopped Griffith-Jones from calling Christine a prostitute even though he had never given any evidence to prove she was.

Chapter 18

Blondes have more fun.

Next was Mandy Rice-Davies. She probably came off best out of all the women who testified. She was more intelligent than Christine and certainly more confident when it came to standing her ground against Griffith-Jones. Mandy is famous for something that happened at the pre-trial hearing, when she was informed by Ward's barrister James Burge that Lord Astor had denied an affair between them, or even having met her, and she made the classic reply, "Well he would, wouldn't he?"

She was still at school when sweet rationing ended. She had listened to Elvis on foreign radio stations because the BBC refused to play his songs. It was television which showed the teenager a world of possibilities. She was one of the first of the sixties generation. In many ways she was lucky to have met Ward in London at the age of sixteen. Another man may have picked up the young girl and things could have been very different.

In the dock she agreed that she had given Ward money when she lived with him in Wimpole Mews for a few weeks. But let's go back a bit first. She did not have the same friendship with Ward that Christine had and had never lived at the flat on a long-term basis. She was originally slum Landlord Peter Rachman's mistress. He got her a flat and paid her some shopping money every week. When he died of a heart attack, she tried to commit suicide and she stayed with Ward in Wimpole Mews, who also let her parents stay while she recovered. She admitted that she had sex with Lord Astor again when he came over to perk her up (the old rascal). But he did not give her any money for it.

She told the court that through Ward she met a businessman by the name of Dr Savundra. She liked him and willingly had sex with him on about five occasions over a period of a few months. He gave her a small amount of money to pay for modelling fees. Strangely, although Dr Emil Savundra was well known to the public (he ended up being involved in a massive vehicle insurance scam) and could easily have been brought in by the prosecution to give his side of the story, he seems to have never been asked. I'm not sure why the defence did not call him either; perhaps they did and he refused to turn up? Even if he had given Mandy money purely for sex, there was no mention of ward organising the deal and deciding the fee. The prosecution argued that what she did with the money afterwards was what Ward was on trial for.

When asked how much she had given Ward when she and her parents had stayed in his flat for a few weeks, Mandy replied that it was a couple of pounds. It was a gesture of thanks. This would not have covered the cost of rent, food, or any of the bills over this period. Griffith-Jones, a man who would not let his servants read certain books, would have known this. He would also have known that Ward had legally earnt around six thousand pounds during this same period. When he tried to push Mandy into admitting she was a prostitute he became more unstuck. This particular lady was not for turning tricks.

Mandy told the jury how she had at first refused to give a statement against Ward because he had done nothing wrong. Then she was arrested for having a provisional driving licence that Rachman had got her from Ireland because it was quicker, and she had never changed it to a British driving licence because she didn't know she had to. For that she was sent to Holloway prison for a couple of weeks. DCI Herbert and Sgt Eustace, the same police officers involved in investigating Ward (and Gordon and Edgecombe) visited her a couple of times. It is not known what was said, as no records have ever been published.

When she was released, she went to go on holiday. She found detective chief inspector Herbert waiting at the airport, and she was further arrested for not paying the hire purchase on a television that Rachman had rented out in his name and then had the temerity to die. Again, nothing to do with her, and legally a civil matter. Herbert could have also spoken to her about the matter while she was in prison. Another blatant abuse of process. Instead, it was a threat of going back to prison if she did not help the police with their enquiries. She agreed. This time she was granted bail for a thousand pounds; due to return the day she was also due to give evidence. She was trapped. Try to leave and it would be prison, not give a statement and it was prison, fail to turn up for court, it would be prison. The police did everything but point a gun at her head to get her to the Old Bailey. When she got there the judge did nothing but hold her up as a target. Even before half time it was pretty much two nil to the prosecution.

~

Of the other "Victims" we have Sally Norrie. The story was that Ward had seen her drinking coffee in a café near Baker Street with her boyfriend, to which Christine lured him away and then pushed Sally into the clutches of Ward who had his wicked way with her (hopefully not over the café table in-between the brown sauce and a sausage sandwich). Technically Christine was either a victim or an accomplice in this offence, as she had (knowingly) lured a Sally away and into the arms of ward. In truth, Sally and Ward had met a few times. He had taken her to Cliveden that weekend in the summer of sixty-one, and at some point, she had consensual sex with him. The relationship faded away, and that was pretty much it. Certainly, Sally did not look back on it with anger.

The judge should have looked at the evidence of this charge and thrown it out. He should have put the detectives in the dock and accused them of wasting his time. Man sees woman, they like each other, meet socially a few times, have sex, realise things are not going to work out long term, move on. The fact that at the start Christine did the "my friend fancies you" routine is hardly cause for the police to get involved let alone a judge in the Old Bailey. Why he didn't throw the charge out is something that only he, a man who was meant to be impartial, can answer.

What is also interesting is how Sally became a victim. There is nothing to suggest she kept in contact with either Ward or Christine. Which means she disappeared at least a year before the police charged Ward. The only way they would have known about her was from Ward when he spoke to MI5 in 1961 because she was at Cliveden. But MI5 had no knowledge of any meetings with Ward, and the man he claimed to have spoken with didn't exist. We must also take it that Sally had never made any complaint to the police in the intervening two years. And so, the government and the police had to go looking for Sally and then had to try and make her story sound like he was a sexual predator.

We should also make note that the police were only concerned with events from around 1961. They could have gone back further and found something a bit more salacious; but even the press are bound by certain rules. Anything that is considered to be evidence in an ongoing criminal investigation is off limits from being published. The police can either serve a D Notice, stopping any item from being published, or release information themselves.

~

The next count was that Ward had procured a young woman of virtue into his lair of desire. She was given anonymity (unlike the others) because bizarrely Griffith-Jones believed she was from a good family. Again, Christine Keeler had asked her to go on a date with Ward. The young woman did. She admitted sleeping with Ward because she liked him. Another crime in which two consenting adults had done the most natural thing in the world in private. Another time in which the man with the wig who sat in judgement of all wrongs should have made the right decision and kicked this charge out. He never. Judge Marshall wanted the prosecution to throw enough mud at Ward to make something stick on the mind's eye of the jury, going against all principles of British justice. The only honest thing about the trial was that at least the next two people to give evidence were real prostitutes.

~

It is here we should talk about policing in the early sixties. Dixon of Dock Green and Heartbeat show coppers there to keep the Queen's Peace. Quite often they were portrayed as a one-man band who knew the name of everyone on his beat. Those that worked in the big cities also knew the names of the local prostitutes.

When it came to a police officer attending court, it was simply a matter of reading from your pocket notebook and answering a few questions. The only forensic evidence was fingerprints. The word of a police officer was taken to be the same as the word of the Queen or the local vicar.

As such, can any historic trial remain pure when viewed through the modern microscope? The answer is yes. Even today we are always going to be at the mercy of individuals willing to lie on oath, witnesses and victims with a secret agenda, and corrupt police officers wanting to send the innocent man to prison, but most of the time the police have done the right thing and jury have got it right. The danger is when the whole of the establishment decides what justice means.

In June 2022 a white male Metropolitan police officer was jailed for twenty weeks after pleading guilty to sending messages in a private group chat two years prior, which someone later found to be offensive. One was of a prayer mat with the face of George Floyd on it. Tasteless, yes, but the image was not illegal. The officer did not show it to the general public and there was no evidence that it affected him doing his job. The white male officer pleaded guilty at court to sending an offensive message. The judge should have noted that WhatsApp is not a public network, but this man, for sending tasteless jokes to some friends, was sent to prison. The establishment clearly wanted to make an example of him.

In 2021, Novlett Williams, a black female superintendent in the Metropolitan police, went to court after sending a video clip of a five-year-old child being abused. This is a criminal offence of possession and distribution of an Indecent Image and carries with it a five-year prison sentence. At her trial in the Old Bailey, she told the jury that her sister had sent it in the hope they would be able to trace the man who was in the clip. She did not inform anyone in the police of the clip. She was found guilty and given 200 hours community service. But the Black Police Association complained that the criminal justice system and the police were institutionally racist. She was subsequently given her job back. In 2022 the Metropolitan police tried to dismiss her again in an internal disciplinary case but again were told that this was a form of racism. She kept her job. The Black Police Officers Association put out the statement: "So glad to hear this verdict and hopefully the Met will allow Robyn to get on with her career in peace. It should never have taken this long, and forces need to stop hounding black officers and staff in a way they wouldn't for the majority of our colleagues."

This scenario highlights that even for those working within law enforcement, if the establishment want to bring you down, they will. And if the establishment wants to keep you up, they will. And if you think that its bad now, imagine what it was like in 1963.

Chapter 19

Miss Whiplash gives the police a good tongue lashing.

Both Ronna Ricardo and Vicki Barrett admitted that they had resorted to prostitution to survive. The prosecution told the jury that Ward had been living off their earnings from January to June 1963, which also happened to be the time that the press had started following Ward and the police started their investigation. So much so that Ward had to move home to get away from the intrusion. And yet no witness had ever seen Ward with these two women. The prosecution got around this conundrum in a rather ingenious way.

Vicki Barrett and Ronna Ricardo had miraculously given statements just a few weeks before the trial started. They said that Ward had arranged for them to sleep with men at his flat in Bryanston Mews. They would turn up and he would take the money and then leave. Sometime later, Vicki or Ronna would turn up, have sex with the man, and leave. Ward promised he would see the women later and give them their share. Both women went on to say in their statements that he never met them afterwards to give them the money. This certainly got around the reason why the press or the police had never seen Ward with either Ronnie Ricardo or Vicki Barrett. Neither could they say how much he owed them. Apparently, this situation went on for weeks, which seems strange as I'm pretty sure most working girls would not put up with that situation. Its lucky that judge Marshall did not add extra offence of theft as well as living off immoral earnings.

The prosecution seemed confident that both women would take the oath and repeat the same spiel about working for Ward and him taking the money. But in the witness box Ricardo broke down in tears and complained that she had been threatened by DCI Herbert. He had told her that if she didn't sign the statement her younger sister would be put into a care home. Whatever Ronna Ricardo was, she could not lie after swearing on the Bible to tell the truth. At this point the judge threatened her to stick to her original statement or she could be imprisoned for contempt of court. She refused. After getting nowhere, the judge told the jury to completely disregard what she had said in the witness box, implying that her statement taken under duress was true, and that she was lying on oath in the Old Bailey. How crazy is that? Ricardo was probably the bravest out of everyone when it really mattered.

Vickie Barrett was a prostitute who gave a statement that she knew Ward shortly after she had been arrested for soliciting on 3rd July 1963, just two weeks before the trial. She claimed that she had spent a few months working for Ward, namely sleeping with men for money, which he kept. She also had stories of making stag films, sex parties with two-way mirrors, light bondage, and a bit of spanking while she was wearing stockings and suspenders. She expressed in detail the horse whips and various toys that she used on men and the two-way mirror installed in Bryanston Mews.

This was all meant to be happening in Wards flat at the time it was under police surveillance. Ward agreed that there was a two-way mirror in the flat between the bedrooms. As for not paying the women their money, Ward was someone who could have been blackmailed if Barrett or Ricardo felt the need, especially as he had been in the news since December. The only truth was that Ward had met Barrett at some point, had used her services, and had drawn a portrait of her. Chances are both women had used the Bryanston Mews flat on previous occasions when it was being run as a knocking shop by Rachmann and De Freitas.

~

After the trial, Vickie Barrett told a reporter that she had lied under oath about Ward. She had met him once when he paid to have sex with her. He was not her pimp, and he was not living on her immoral earnings. She had been set up by the police just to get Ward, and now felt her life was in danger.

The reporter took her back to her address to get her belongings. Vickie went into an address, and then seemingly disappeared. After a while another person came and told the reporter that Vickie had changed her mind. She wasn't going anywhere and wasn't going to speak to anyone. Ward was dead, so what did it matter. The reporter tried a few times to contact Vickie but never got an answer. Since 1963 she has never been seen again.

Hannah Tailford and Francis Brown were also prostitutes. Although not part of any indictment, they had been called to give evidence as witnesses for the prosecution. The main thrust of their evidence was that Ward had tried to set them up with men, to which he would take the money and give the women their share later. Francis gave evidence in the trial that she had been picked up by Ward while she was walking the streets, and that he paid to have sex with her. She spoke about sex parties and photographs taken behind a two-way mirror. Whether this was the address of Bryanston Mews or another we don't know.

Hannah gave evidence of a similar nature. She too had been picked up by Ward and had sex with him. She spoke about driving out of London (possibly Borehamwood) to make blue films. She also said that Ward had supplied her and other women to be at an orgy organised by Prince Philip's cousin the Marquis of Milford Haven. We do not know what else they knew as the judge would quickly shut them down when they wandered off script.

Soon after the trial, the two women also disappeared like Vickie, even though the press were offering substantial sums of money for more stories. Both were to turn up later in a far more sinister fashion.

The Hammersmith nude murders took place in London between 1959 and 1965, where eight prostitutes had been found naked in London, usually strangled. Hannah Tailford was found in February 1964 on the shore of the Thames. She had been strangled, several of her teeth were missing, and her underwear had been stuffed into her mouth. Also in 1964, Francis Brown was found naked in a car park in Kensington. She had also been strangled.

All the women killed were believed to have been murdered in one place, stored for a day or two, then dumped in another place. Why someone would carry out such a flagrant way of disposing of a body when they had taken so much time and effort to hide it after the killing seems very strange. They women could have been dumped in the Thames or the countryside to give the killer more time to dispose of any evidence. Perhaps the killer, or killers, wanted the bodies to be found. There were rumours that all the women had been involved in exclusive parties and blue movies. That's quite a coincidence. Even more of a coincidence was that two of the victims had given evidence in the Ward trial. Whether they and the other women knew more about Ward and his friends is something we shall never know.

~

The artist Vasco Lazzolo gave evidence for the defence. He had been a friend of Ward's for a few years. Both had attended the Thursday club in the late fifties (when Lazzolo did a bronze bust of Prince Phillip), and both had been regular attendees of numerous orgies. Both were interested in art and photography, with Lazzolo rumoured to have an extensive collection of pornographic photographs, some of which he shared with Ward. His evidence did not really help, as he was quite happy to state on oath that he too had enjoyed the company of some of the prostitutes who had appeared in the trial as well. Whether he was also involved in the headless duchess scandal we do not know. Vasco simply wanted it to be known that Ward had never lived off immoral earnings.

Noel Howard-Jones also gave evidence for Ward, saying he was a very kind man who was willing to help anybody. The prosecution dismissed him because he also admitted to having sex with Keeler while they were in a relationship. They never asked him if he had ever paid for sex with her because they knew he had not. As for the other friends over the years that Ward had hoped would come to his rescue…well, there was no one else. Not one of his more influential friends turned up to be a character witness. The judge would later tell the jury that it proved more than all the evidence that Ward was guilty. Men of such esteem and honour would never let a friend down if he was innocent.

The elusive Mr Woods from MI5 never appeared to explain Ward's role in helping the country. Again, the judge told the jury that Ward was just a fantasist who believed he was a spy. The defence found it difficult to argue the case, as Ward had not kept any written records which could corroborate his accounts. When the Secret Service go after one individual, it's difficult to fight back.

None of Wards more famous patients turned up to support him, which the jury could take that perhaps he was not as good with his hands as he liked to think he was, and that he might have had other means of keeping up the lifestyle he was accustomed to.

Detective Chief Inspector Herbert gave evidence. Here was a police officer who had so far been accused of threatening two of the witnesses with prison, forcing one to give evidence otherwise he would send her younger sister to a care home, got a prostitute to be a witness two weeks before the trial; and had not only obstructed the investigation of Lucky Gordon, but had done nothing when Christine had lied in that trial. Thank God the Metropolitan Police have changed since 1963.

He denied any government impropriety. Like Adolf Eichmann, he was just doing his job. When Burge asked him if it was normal for a detective chief inspector to go and personally arrest Mandy at an airport for being in a relationship with a man now dead that had rented a television and she had no idea about it, he replied "Yes". Scotland Yard must have had a really good record of solving crime that year.

~

For Ward in 1963, he must have wondered why the whole world had turned against him. The fifties had been great. The parties, the young women, the freedom to do what he wanted. He was even able to have a political opinion that may have been different from others, but no one was calling for him to be arrested or lose his career. He was to find out the hard way that times had changed. The police were allowed to go after him because the establishment wanted it to happen. After swearing on the Bible to say he was innocent, the son of a vicar had suddenly become God's loneliest man.

Chapter 20.

Summing up and coming down.

Ward gave an honest account when he stood in the dock. He knew all the women. He had slept with most of them, some of which he knew were prostitutes. But he made it clear he had never committed any of the offences he had been charged with, especially when it came to living off immoral earnings. Unlike the police who had taken months to gather evidence Ward had only been given a matter of weeks to remember what happened two years ago. The trial had been rushed into court because the prosecution was desperate to finish it quickly.

Just a few months prior, Lucky Gordon had been sentenced to three years in prison on false evidence, namely that Christine Keller had lied on oath that he assaulted her. Quite probably he deserved to be punished after he had hit and raped her on several previous occasions. So, we may not have been too bothered about him doing time but a man is put on trial for the offence he has believed to have committed, and Christine had only given a statement about the assault.

Gordon's defence was that he was somewhere else at the time, and there were two people who could prove his innocence. The police did not bother to find them. It may have been that as the two men were black neither they nor the police were in too much of a hurry to chat to each other. But reporters also had Christine in a taped interview saying she had lied on oath about who had assaulted her. Gordon's defence barrister submitted the appeal on the day he had been convicted. There is a time limit on when an appeal must be initially heard, and that limit would be reached on Tuesday 30th July. The trial against Stephen Ward was quickly booked into the Old Bailey, with the prosecution hoping to be finished by the 29th. Unfortunately, due to some of the victims claiming that they had been forced to give evidence that trial had overran by a few days.

The two witnesses were found and gave statements confirming Gordon's innocence. Another witness at the party now said it wasn't Gordon. The tape recording had been handed over with confirmation that it was Christine's voice and her saying it wasn't Gordon. A selection of independent judges went through the evidence and agreed that Cristine Keeler had lied in court on oath. Judge Marshall was informed on Tuesday morning that Keeler had lied during a previous trial and had therefore committed perjury. She had also taken the oath in the Ward trial and been asked by Burge if she had told the truth in the Gordon trial, to which she replied "Yes." So now this was two counts of perjury. As she was a witness in three of the five indictments against Ward, it should have been enough to throw the case out.

Judge Marshal should have officially informed both barristers as soon as he was given the news. He didn't. At this point the Ward trial should have been stopped. It wasn't. Christine should have been arrested and her evidence (and the indictment against Ward) dismissed. It wasn't. The jury should have been informed that she had lied on oath on a previous occasion and therefore what she had said in this trial should be treated as unreliable. It wasn't. The trial crept on with a judge at the highest court in the land refusing to do what not only is right but also what is the law. And we have a barrister so desperate to see Ward convicted that he was willing to go against every principle of what a fair trial should be. Burge could only be directed to inform the jury of the situation by order of the judge, but Marshall did not feel it was worth saying anything just yet.

Burge made his summing up short and succinct. There was no evidence to show that Christine and Mandy were prostitutes. There was no evidence to say that Ward was living off their immoral earnings. There was no evidence that Ward had forced Christine to procure two young women and coercing them into having sex with him. As for the other prostitutes, it was agreed that Ward had slept with them but did not live off their earnings. It should be mentioned that a collection of erotic photographs had been found in Ward's flat, which he admitted to owning. But they were never produced in court and the full details of them are not known. Burge informed the jury that in the eyes of the law Ward had not committed any of the offences within their legal definition. Whether or not his personal life was distasteful didn't matter. Ward may have been a sinner, but he was not a criminal.

The circus of deception started again when the prosecution gave his summing up. Griffith-Jones pointed out in his closing speech that Stephen Ward was "a thoroughly filthy fellow and "thoroughly immoral". It was a persistent tide of abuse towards the defendant that had no bearing on the case. It is only when a person is found guilty and convicted that the judge can make comments about the defendant's morality (or lack of it). This was breached by Griffiths-Jones, and he should have been reprimanded, but he wasn't.

Why the judge failed to disclose information that Keeler had lied in the trial is not just a mystery, it's an offence. Someone must have ordered him not to. The jury was only made aware later in the evening that Lucky Gordon's conviction had been quashed because it was in the news. The judge and the prosecution barrister had forgotten that the plebs were allowed to be informed of important events. The press reported that Christine Keeler could be liable to be arrested for perjury in the Gordon trial. The jury knew that Christine had stood in the witness box and said she had told the truth when giving evidence in that trial. They must have gone into court the next morning wondering if was all over. But the judge had spent the night deciding how he was going to phrase the situation in his own summing up. It was a work of genius.

Judge Marshall said to the jury that even though Christine had lied on oath in a previous trial (and ended up getting an innocent man three years in prison), it was testament to her character that she was willing to come forward and tell the truth now (even though she had clearly lied again). This was an outrageous thing to say, as it implied that Christine was telling the truth and Stephen Ward was lying. The words from Judge Marshall made the jury believe that Ward must be guilty beyond all reasonable doubt. Somebody wanted Ward sent to prison even though he was innocent.

~

With the benefit of hindsight there is an argument that Ward bordered on what we would now call grooming. If Christine and Mandy had been in their mid-twenties, had seen a bit more of the world, were a bit more mature emotionally, we might have said that they entered the relationship fully aware of what was happening. Most of the jury would have been men and women in their forties and fifties, possibly with children the same age as Mandy and Christine. If Ward had not admitted to sleeping with prostitutes he might have been seen as an artist looking for his muse.

The prosecution knew that sleeping with a prostitute was more offensive in the publics eyes than living off immoral earnings. They kept taking down his character, rather than his actions. If ward was capable of asking anyone for sex, would you leave him alone with your wife or your daughter? We can go further and say that most of the jury believed that their betters (namely the judge and the prosecution barrister) would guide them towards the correct decision.

And here is the great irony. For all his libertarian values Ward was distinctly from the English old school. Up to now he had tried to do everything by the book. He believed that what happened behind closed doors should stay behind closed doors. That you never told tales and never ratted on your friends. He was ideal establishment fodder because he too believed the establishment was essentially right. When caught, Ward did what he believed to be the decent thing and said nothing. He had tried to do what was right in the eyes of his friends, his fellow peers, his country, the justice system, the jury, and on the Bible; only to find that the establishment were going to crucify him no matter what he did.

~

Standing there in the box listening to a judge tell the jury that Christine, having lied on oath in both a previous trial and in this one, was somehow virtuous, must have been a shattering blow. Since the moment of his arrest, Ward believed he would be found innocent. But on that Wednesday afternoon when at the end of his summing up Judge Marshall told to jury to remember the fact that Ward had been abandoned by his (powerful) friends at such an important time was because they too must have also believed he was guilty, it must have been a bitter personal blow.

The judge went on to say that during this investigation the Metropolitan police had acted beyond reproach and had acted above and beyond their duties to bring such a heinous criminal to justice. This was after Christine Keeler, Mandy Rice-Davies, Ronna Ricardo and Vickie Barrett had all confessed in the witness box that they had been forced to give their accounts for fear of police threats. It was also after the same detectives involved in the Lucky Gordon trial had taken him to court and watched him get three years even though they knew he was innocent, and that Christine had lied on oath in that trial and had lied on oath in this one.

But when the establishment wants to persecute you, the letter of the law becomes a fictional story. You are going to be portrayed as the villain no matter what you say and do. The prosecution knew they would lose if they simply relied on constructing a narrative on legal terms; so, they did their best during the trial to guide to jury into making decisions based on emotions rather than facts. The same barrister who had wanted to ban the novel Lady Chatterley's Lover, now used language to try and hide the truth of a man's life.

Stephen Ward had sat through the Eichmann trial in Jerusalem a few years before and watched a guilty man who tried to blame the system. Now here was Ward, an innocent man being accused by the system. He had become nothing more than a problem that needed to disappear, something to be discarded as if the value of his life did not matter. More importantly, the establishment could not take another scandal. They needed to make him a scapegoat, an example to others that there would be no more honeytraps. At that point Ward realised the whole system believed he knew too much. Worse, they didn't know if he could be trusted; and it gave him no hope for the future. The sense of an ending that had been following him since the summer of nineteen-sixty-one had finally arrived in Court One of the Old Bailey.

Strangely, at the end of the afternoon the judge did not cancel Ward's bail. In most criminal cases in which a custodial sentence is likely, especially if the judge has already started his summing up, the judge can put restrictions on the defendant, such as only being allowed at one address and not leaving until the next morning or even spending the night in custody. Ironically, if the judge had been as harsh with the rules as he had with his language it might have saved Ward's life. The judge informed the court that he would finish his speech in the morning.

That night, due to the number of reporters in Bryanston Mews, Ward stayed at Howard-Jones' flat. He wrote a series of letters. One of them was to Vickie Barrett:

"*I don't know what it was or who it was that made you do what you did. But if you have any decency left, you should tell the truth like Ronna Riccardo. You owe this not to me, but to everyone who may be treated like you or like me in the future.*"

It is then believed that at some point in the night Ward decided to take his own life. But new evidence suggests that may not be the case.

PART FIVE

I have neither eyes to see, nor tongue to speak.

Chapter 21.

Aftermath.

Let it be Beatle-esque.

When does a man decide to take his own life? Is there a specific moment when they know they are planning to die. You think about it. You get ready. You buy the pills, find the rope, walk to the train tracks. And then there is the precious seconds, minutes, hours, days, weeks, months, years before you make the final decision. How do you decide that it is better to be dead and free than carry on living and be in pain? Is it a rational thought, a moment of truly clear consciousness; or is it a slow build-up of broken moments in our brain which eventually black out our minds-eye? How did we build the pyramids, create great works of art, understand the wonders of nature, land on the moon, and yet not be able to save those who feel that life is not worth living anymore?

Eighteen people kill themselves every day in this country. Suicide is three times higher in men than women. The most common method for men is hanging. The same idea that Judas had has lasted longer than Christianity itself. Poisoning is next, which is an overdose by any other name. This includes the use of prescribed and over the counter medication usually washed down with alcohol. We know that booze is a depressant. For some it starts off as a way of being sociable, then as a way of getting legless, then numbing the pain, until finally it becomes your only friend at night and the only thing that gets you through the next day. Men also tend to write shorter suicide notes. Well, not quite.

30th July 4.30pm. After listening to the first half of judge Marshall's damning summing-up to the jury, in which he said he expected them all to find the defendant guilty, Ward was released from court. He had been staying with his friend Noel Howard-Jones during the trial to hide from the press. The flat was in Mallord Street, Chelsea, not far from the river Thames and Sloane Square tube station.

On the way back he asked a friend to stop outside Harrods and handed over a prescription. As a doctor he was allowed to carry a prescription pad and would be able to administer drugs to anyone, including himself. The friend went inside and up to the chemists counter. He found out later he had got a packet of barbiturates, which Ward had been using since the start of the trial to help him sleep.

That evening inside the flat, Ward spent some time writing a series of short letters, which he sealed and then asked Howard-Jones to send them with the proviso: "Only if I am convicted and sent to prison." These do not sound like the words of a man about to commit suicide.

We could argue that the messages were his way of letting people know that they had let him down and that he might have more to say when he was given a suspended sentence, in prison, or even when finally released…If we knew what he had written, and to whom. It is believed he wrote about ten of these letters. It seems rather a lot of work for someone about to commit suicide, especially as he then had a meal with his current partner the 22-year-old Julie Gulliver, and Howard-Jones.

Later that evening the reporter Tom Mangold came to the flat. Mangold worked for The Daily Express and had guarded Ward throughout the trial, as the paper wanted an exclusive story once it was over and didn't want ward speaking to anyone else. Mangold was asked by Ward to hand deliver the letters. He said "No". Mangold then states Ward handed him a letter on the condition he would not open it until he was dead. This could be taken two ways. A man at the centre of a witch hunt by the establishment may believe his life might be in danger once he was confined in a building full of criminals (prison, not parliament). Or he was going to take his own life if he was found guilty and given a custodial sentence. Mangold took this letter and left. We do not know if anyone else in the flat had heard Ward's comment.

Also, with Mangold that night was press photographer Brian Wharton. He says that Ward was angrier than upset about the way the trial was going. He told Wharton he was writing to the Home Secretary and that he would "Name names". Wharton then agreed with Ward to collect him in the morning so they could drive up to Westminster and Ward could be photographed dropping the letter off at the Home Secretaries office. Wharton took pictures of Ward that evening as he wrote the letters. It is not known if those letters could be seen in the photographs, or the details of who they were for; or if Ward meant the letter that was going to the Home Secretary. Wharton left, then drove to the Daily Express building in Fleet Street. He went inside and dropped off the roll of film to be processed. It is not known what time he was in the building, but we can assume it was late enough for most of the staff to have gone home.

Ward spent the rest of the evening in the flat with Julie Gulliver and Howard-Jones. At around 11pm Howard-Jones went to bed and Ward left to drive Gulliver home to her own flat in Bayswater just a few minutes away. There then appears to be a concerning black hole in the time frame that no one is able to explain.

Howard-Jones believes he was woken up about 1am by the front door opening. He then went straight back to sleep. Again, he had no concerns about Ward's behaviour and the letters he had written a few hours ago, in which Howard-Jones must have been present.

The official story is that during the night Ward sat and wrote his last letter to Howard-Jones.

"I am sorry I had to do this here. It is really more than I can stand – the horror, day after day, at court and in the streets. It is not only fear, it is a wish not to let them get me. I would rather get myself. I do hope I have not let people down too much. I tried to do my stuff but after Marshall's summing up. I've given up all hope. The car needs oil in the gear-box by the way, be happy in it. Incidentally, it was surprisingly easy and required no guts. I am sorry to disappoint the vultures. I only hope this has done the job. Delay resuscitation as long as possible."

Howard Jones was woken at 8.30am when he heard the telephone ringing and expected Ward to answer it. It kept ringing. Howard-Jones went out of his bedroom and found Ward slumped unconscious in the living room. He rang for an ambulance. When it arrived, a different photographer was already waiting outside. Ward, the son of a vicar, was taken to St. Stephens Hospital, where he remained in a coma.

Just like Saint Alban being the first Christian martyr in England, Saint Stephen was the first Christian martyr in the world. It appears patterns of persecution had been following Ward all of his life.

Back at the Old Bailey that morning, while Ward was in hospital, judge Marshall took the decision to continue with his summing up, adding ruefully that attempted suicide was the last refuge of a scoundrel. His summing up took a total of five hours, far longer than any normal summing up. The jury took less time than that to come back than those involved in the Simpson trial and decided Ward was guilty of only two of the counts: that of living off the immoral earnings of Christine Keeler and living off the immoral earnings of Mandy Rice-Davies.

Here is the punch in the gut that had troubled Ward throughout the trial. Both women had said they had only given money to help toward a phone bill. That was it. Neither could recall giving him money for anything else, neither claimed to be prostitutes. Although ward did not know it, for the other offences the jury found him not guilty. They must have felt they needed to charge him with something. Ironically, the offence of living off immoral earnings carried a maximum seven-year sentence. The judge listened to the jury, then declined from sentencing Ward until he had recovered.

That morning, when Brian Wharton went to the Daily Express building, he was told his roll of film had disappeared. As it was late at night, it could not have been a member of staff. Had someone followed Wharton and then had the power to get into the building and take the negatives? The letter Ward had written to the Home Secretary is classified under the Official Secrets Act and will not be released to the public until 2071. We do not even know if it was written by Ward. If it was, we don't know what is in it. Why someone has decided to would be nearly a hundred years before it could be looked at must have come from someone high up in the government.

Ward was taken to hospital and did not regain consciousness. He died three days later, on Saturday 3rd August 1963. And this ends the official version of events.

~

There are a few things that we need to discuss. The first is the state of Ward's mental health. He went to trial believing he was innocent; and no doubt would be found not guilty. A jury had to believe beyond all reasonable doubt that Ward had committed the offences he had been charged with. Looking at the evidence, including the knowledge that Christine had lied under oath, Ward might have been down, but he certainly wasn't beaten. Even if Lucky Gordon's appeal had been delayed, Ward knew it would have still affected any decision in his own trial at a later date.

What must have hurt in that first week were the accusations about his morality. Ward believed he had always acted like a gentleman towards women. Whatever our views on prostitution, Ward saw nothing wrong in sleeping with a woman and paying for the privilege. He did not want to be in a long-term relationship and thought this was the ideal situation. From a modern perspective, if these had been women he had met on a dating app, paid for a mela, had sex, then left, would it be any different?

I wonder if there was a point when standing in the dock, Ward realised that he was finally getting fucked by the establishment. Was that the start of a breakdown, or, like the philosopher Albert Camus, can you make a rational decision that when weighed and measured by any means, such as happiness or health, the amount of time you have left will never be as good as the life you have already lived?

What if you include those moments when you start forgetting things more often. The idea of the brain going before the heart has become more prevalent in modern times. It is believed the comedian

Robin Williams killed himself because he was suffering from a form of dementia. Within a few years he would have been unable to remember his name and struggled to walk and talk. The man who had made millions of people laugh and who had beaten alcohol and cocaine addiction knew he was never going to beat losing his sense of humour.

Ward's state of mind that night must also include the knowledge that like all of us from the moment we are born we are dying at a rate of twenty-four hours per day. I don't know what his physical health was like in 1963, but he probably had reached the age where he had to sit down to put his socks on. He wasn't sleeping, but that could have been going on for years. Alcohol and smoking would be taking their toll. The long-term use of barbiturates may have also affected his mind. They would have also affected him physically, as he may have built up a resilience to them.

It seems strange that Ward was still writing when other people were in the flat. The photographer Wharton commented that Ward was writing his letter to the home secretary while he was there. Would a man contemplating on killing himself write to someone he barely knew, and do it in front of so many people?

Moving on to look at the suicide note. Or rather, suicide notes, as ward appeared to have written a few. Or, more precisely, let's not. We can't. I have never seen a copy of the original note, or any others, so I cannot compare the writing to any previous handwriting by Ward. Instead, we are left to look at the words themselves to what is considered the main suicide note.

"I'm sorry to disappoint the vultures. I feel the day is lost. The ritual sacrifice is demanded and I cannot face it".

It certainly seems to be the grammar of a well-educated person.

The bit about the "Day" no doubt refers to judge Marshall's summing up and his comment that if Ward was innocent his friends in high places would have come to his aid. On that day Ward had called out 'No' to protest about some of the comments the judge had made against him. The judge warned him about his behaviour, and Ward apologised to the court, telling everyone it had all been a great strain.

Prosecution barrister Griffith-Jones quickly stood up and announced to the jury that of course it was a great strain…for a guilty man to hear the truth at last.

These comments would have been heard by anyone in the gallery and could have been reported in the evening papers. It is also possible that Ward could have met someone that night and told them. Finally, this suicide note refers to someone who is going to end it all…we just don't know if Ward wrote the words.

There was also another note with the collection of sealed envelopes. This was for Howard-Jones. Ward wanted him to deliver the envelopes if he was convicted and sent to prison. Why would someone write a suicide note and another note asking for letters to be delivered to those named if you thought you were going to jail?

There is a report that the writing in one suicide note became extremely disjointed as the drugs began to work, with the sentence even trailing off at the end as he collapsed. Wouldn't you write the suicide note before the drugs and alcohol took hold? It all seems rather strange given that as a medical man he would know exactly how many pills to take to end his own life.

Since his death other people have come forward to say that after Ward had dropped his partner off, he then met someone from the Secret Service. There are two hours from dropping off his partner and returning to the flat that we cannot account for. Would the police, after months of spying on him, really take the night off knowing he might leave the country?

It's believed the person Ward met also came back to the flat with him around 1am. Howard-Jones was asleep. The person has then helped Ward take some pills to help him sleep, then maybe some more. They just didn't know how many would kill him. The suicide note was written before Ward lost consciousness. Its plausible. It's possible, but it's also a massive risk. What possible reason could there be?

It turns out there are a few.

Ward had spoken to the Secret Service agent codenamed "Woods" about Ivanov before Cliveden, and about Profumo afterwards. How many meetings they had has never been confirmed. No doubt Ward had also passed on other stories he had heard at various parties that he took Ivanov to. During the Cuban missile crisis, Ward was in contact with high-ranking officials from England, Russia, and America. All this from a man of supposed loose morals. The scandal of Ward being the liaison officer during the day and a sexual louche at night would be an international disgrace. After the missile crisis the cold war heated up considerably. England was looking towards the General Election. Kennedy was campaigning for a second term. The CIA did not have enough influence to control the press in England, and if newspapers were to publish stories about Ward, women, and Kennedy (and others), it would be a disaster. Did the Secret Service, the CIA, or even the Russian KGB want ward to stay silent: Yes. Would they seriously consider killing him to keep him silent on a permanent basis? Possibly.

What about the national political aspect. MP's such as Cyril Smith were involved child sex abuse during this time and it may have been covered up by Westminster. Ten years later Jeremy Thorpe was involved in the murder of his homosexual lover while trying to become leader of the Liberal Party, and the establishment didn't seem to have a problem with this. Thirty years later, prime minister Tony Blair used the fake dossier on weapons of mass destruction to start a war in Iraq, killing thousands of women and children. It appears that some politicians are willing to do anything to stay in power. It would not be unreasonable to suggest that a politician who had attended one of Ward's parties was now extremely concerned that they could be exposed if Ward mentioned their name or had photographic evidence. There would be no better moment to get rid of the problem than now. The issue would be finding someone used to getting their hands dirty.

The Hammersmith Nudes Murders have a closer link to Stephen Ward than we realise. The first murder was believed to have taken place in 1959, it was not until early 1964 that the killings really began. All eight women were either prostitutes or known to have made Stag Movies, but it is not clear if these were soft porn for the British market or full-on hardcore sex for the more exclusive clients. The production team behind such movies didn't like to give their details due to not wanting to be arrested, so we do not know if the women were taken to Borehamwood to be filmed or were made to take their clothes off somewhere else. The same team of detective who had investigated Ward and everyone else at his trial, were also tasked to investigate these murders, which remain unsolved to this day. All murders took place in London, near to the River Thames, and Hammersmith,

Elizabeth Figg. Killed in June 1959

Gwynneth Rees. Killed in September 1963 (few weeks after the Ward trial).

Hannah Tailford. Killed April 1964.

Helen Barthelemy. Killed April 1964.

Mary Fleming. Killed July 1964.

Frances Brown. Killed October 1964 (she had given evidence in Ward's trial).

Bridget O'Hara. Killed February 1965.

Had all of them met Ward at some point, had they been involved in one of his parties, did they know secrets?

Although all the murders have never been solved, even at the time there were rumours that a police officer, possibly two police officers were involved in the women's deaths.

Another rumour was that Ward had met someone because they were looking for photographs which were extremely incriminating to a person high up in the establishment. Ward was clever enough not to keep that sort of thing lying around and probably had them hidden in a bank vault. He wasn't about to expose where they were no matter how many pills were slipped into his drink.

The nearest bank vault to Ward was just off Baker Street. If he was going to hide any secrets, it would be underground. The rule of law is that if no one visits their safety deposit box in seven years, the bank will inform the government in the belief that the person may have died. The government can then make an application to the court to open the box, but this would be a matter of public record. If only there was a different way...

~

In September 1971, over seven years after Ward had died, a team of criminals came up with an ingenious plan to rent a shop near Barclays Bank in Bakers Street. The plan was to dig into the basement and make a tunnel to break into the banks vault and its safety deposit boxes. The film about the heist, called *The Bank Job,* was released in 2012. The story in the film is that MI5 and the government were involved because there were after photographs of a member of the royal family in compromising positions. The film also shows a link between a corrupt police officer, Peter Rachman's enforcer Michael de Freitas, a woman and two black men.

The film hints that the woman in the photographs were of Princess Margaret enjoying herself on holiday in the Caribbean, but what if the rumour was only half true? What if the government were after pictures of a different member of the royal family, and this one happened to have been friends with Stephen Ward.

Michael de Freitas, who also called himself Michael X, lent Ward the use of Rachman's flat in Bryanston Mews in the last few months before he died. This was the flat with the two-way mirror built into a bedroom wall. Did ward happen to mention some incriminating photographs? And Let's not forget DCI Herbert, a copper allegedly so bent he couldn't even lie straight in bed.

In the film the group were almost caught when an amateur radio ham listened in to them speaking to each other on their walkie-talkies. The man went to the police, who questioned him about unlawfully listening in to private broadcasts. Because the man refused to be silenced, the police went to the bank, but as the vault door was on a time lock and could not be opened until Monday they simply walked away. How true this is, we do not know.

What is true is that after the bank vault had been broken into, the government stepped in with a D-Notice. This is a Defence Notice, which stops any reporting of certain situations for reasons of national security. This was usually done in times of a national crisis or to keep government secrets safe, not holiday snaps. And as there was total anonymity in relation to who owned the safety boxes, why would the government stop any reporting on the robbery unless they already knew what was in the vaults, more specifically, one box in particular? The main people involved in the bank job were paid off and given immunity on the basis they never spoke about what happened. Princess Margaret died in 2002. It would certainly have been easier to promote a fake rumour than a real one which included any members of the royal family that were still alive then.

~

Back in 1963, when the jury returned to Court 1 of the Old Bailey and informed that Ward was in hospital, Judge Marshall refused to adjourn the trial. If The Suicide Act of 1961 had stopped it being a criminal offence, the good judge would probably have added another charge to the list. Instead, he ordered that Ward be put into custody by having the police guard him twenty-four hours a day, which also stopped any public visitors from seeing how he was getting on (other police officers, and Government workers could see him in secret).

The hospital had been informed of what drugs Ward was believed to have taken and did their best to get him to recover. And he should have. He had not taken enough pills to cause his vital organs to stop working. They found it strange that the quantity in his system did not match the condition he was in. He had been found while still half conscious, indicating he had taken the drugs less than four hours from when he was found. The amount in his stomach was not considered fatal (although he may have taken some the night before). But for some reason his body just continued to break down while he was in hospital, even though he was now under the constant watch of the police. It is said that Ward never regained consciousness. This is also strange, as he should have recovered within twenty-four hours. He died three days later, after the jury had found him guilty in his absence.

At the post-mortem it was believed that Ward had ingested between ten and twelve tablets of Nembutal, which was not enough to kill him. As it was listed as a suicide (proved by the suicide note) there was no need for a full autopsy to be done. As such, any other chemicals in his body, or any marks on his body, were never recorded as being part of the cause of death.

Based on the police report, the coroner at the inquest put Ward's death down as suicide. There was no need to carry out any further enquiries. The whole process, from the moment he had been found unconscious to the moment he was cremated had been done with excessive haste and little regard for any wider investigation into how a man had died. For Ward, who had spent years trying to get complimentary medicine to be given its proper status in helping to heal both mind and body, it was the final insult.

Chapter 22.

Two thousand light years from home.

Things just seemed to go wrong too many times
    (Tony Hancock's suicide note*)*

There is an interesting incident that happened on the weekend in-between the trial. A small London gallery was displaying Ward's collection of portraits. These drawings included pictures of Prince Phillip and Princes Margaret. Barely looking around, a man walked in and bought the lot, over a hundred rough sketches, and paid in today's money about a quarter of a million pounds for what was the work of an amateur artist. It has never been made public who the man was, who paid for the pictures (a bankers draft does not have to name the account), or where they ended up. This was also before any decision had been made in the trial. If someone was trying to make a good business investment, how come they never sold them after Ward had died, and how did they know he wasn't going to make the end of the week? The pictures, including those of Prince Philip, simply disappeared.

Ward went into the second week of the trial a very rich man, but his finances have always been a bit of a mystery. During the trial he admitted he had borrowed money from various people, including Christine and Mandy, but always paid them back. In the days before credit cards and cash machines a man either paid by cheque or went to the bank to draw out his money. Ward did not have a gambling habit or debts to pay off, he was one of those people just didn't seem to understand or care about his finances. But as with any addiction, years of avoiding your financial situation will catch up with you in the end.

One of the main causes of suicide is depression, often caused by money troubles. Some men see their status as defined by wealth. A better job, better car, better clothes, better home, give them a sense of worth. To lose it through bankruptcy, retirement, or unemployment, can make some feel like less of a man. And when you reach a certain age, it is difficult to start all over again. As someone once said, life is what happens when you're busy making other plans. If Ward had been found not guilty, or even gone to prison, what would he have done then? Become a caricature artist for tourists in Lond, go back to America, write his memoirs?

Ward's funeral was held in secret with only a few people turning up for a man whose life had revolved around social gatherings. The writer John Osborne had a wreath of white roses made with the message "To Stephen Ward, a victim of British hypocrisy."

After Ward died there were more lurid stories. But these were not about his life or the political corruption that killed him. It seemed that people were more interested in the debauched upper-class orgies than any miscarriage of justice. Who did what to whom, how many times, and who else was there, were the headlines everyone fingered the newspapers for.

~

As time marched on, Ward became a footnote in the Profumo scandal. The person who had introduced Christine to Profumo and Ivanov at the swimming pool had somehow managed to be the one who drowned under the weight of history. The government stopped any investigations by the newspapers by declaring that Lord Denning was going to carry out his own inquiry and promised to publish the report, leaving journalists to wait…and wait…and wait, as the government inquiry moved at a petty pace from day to day. There would also be other things that happened this year to distract the public.

Just a few days after Ward's death, The Great Train Robbery took place on 8th August 1963. A load of likely lads from London worked out that the best way to stop a train was to cover the bulb of a green lamp with a black glove and then hook up a red lamp to a battery and place it by the tracks. The train was filled with cash that couldn't be traced. The robbers used a bit of shouting and pushing but no guns. One of the engineers got hit on the head; but the other eighty men on the train were not hurt. Within fifteen minutes the robbers had taken cash with today's value of about sixty million pounds. A lot of working-class people publicly cheered them. They had taken money that belonged to the government and had done it so easily that everyone else wondered why they paid their taxes.

But be careful who you make fun of. A government ridiculed will use every means at its disposal to shaft you. The establishment decided to make an example of the robbers (the early sixties seem to have a lot of cases where the establishment wanted to punish the poor). A team of detectives were set up to catch them. Ironically it was the solicitor Brian Field, the one closest to the establishment who gave the game away. His job was to burn down the farm after the gang had finished with it, but he messed up and didn't go. The farm was found, along with fingerprints. At court the men were given sentences of up to thirty years each. The only one who got off lightly was Brian Field, who ended up only doing five years for a sixty-million-pound robbery. Perhaps it was more than a bit of luck that helped the police.

Around the same time a young girl named Pauline Reade was tortured and killed by Ian Brady and Myra Hindley. They went on to torture and kill other children, gaining a sadistic pleasure from recording the abuse. The Moors Murderers would later receive life sentences, as hanging had been abolished between their arrest and conviction. For some it seemed as though the establishment believed that stealing their money should carry the same level of prison time as someone who had taken a child's life.

Perhaps there was too much news that summer. The Beatles and The Rolling Stones seemed to be in the papers every week. The war had ended eighteen years ago, and the country was about to face one of the largest numbers of people to leave school, go to college or university rather than National Service, apply for jobs and join the new world. Although there were others were still trapped in the old system.

After giving evidence to Lord Denning for his report, Christine was given nine months imprisonment for perjury (for lying in Lucky Gordon's trial, not in the Ward trial as all appeals were blocked). Lord Denning, a man who believed that black people should not serve on a jury as their values were not the same as native Englishmen, said he wasn't going to whitewash the inquiry. He interviewed many of his friends…no, sorry; he interviewed numerous people in government to see if they had been involved in any sex scandals, or if any sensitive information had been given to the Ward. Satisfied with his own conscience, he was ready to publish without the need to worry about the Obscene Publications Act.

When the report was published on 26th September it seemed to focus more on Ward as the organiser of sex parties than the exposure of any government secrets. Its findings were that no member of the cabinet was involved in any orgies, no politician had acted improperly either in or out of office, and the establishment had behaved impeccably at all times between 1961 and 1963. Ward was deemed to be an utterly immoral middle-class man and a first-class shit.

Denning stated there was no truth in Ward being advised by the Secret Service to find out about Ivanov (which was wrong). The trial had been carried out with integrity and the conviction had been correct (wrong). Profumo was said to have made a minor error in lying to the House of Commons (also wrong). And there were no issues with him sleeping with a woman who was also sleeping with a Russian spy. As far as the government was concerned this sordid little affair was all done and dusted. There was hardly any fuss from the Labour Party. The reason being was Lord Denning had continually stated that the word "politician" applied to those from all parties, and no one wanted to bring up possible scandals on their own side with an election coming.

The press was not happy with the report. There were comments that Denning had essentially covered up the inquiry to help his friends in parliament keep their jobs. He replied, "While the public interest demands that the facts should be ascertained as completely as possible, there is a higher interest to be considered, namely the interest of justice to the individual which overrides all others".

This was a complete lie as Denning had sacrificed Ward to save the establishment. History shows us that some individuals are bound up with the fate of the universe no matter what they do.

22nd November 1963. Another death was played out with another politician who liked the ladies, another man who had communist friends, and another police investigation where the defendant did not live long enough to see themselves be convicted. There were also rumours of another government cover up. When Lee Harvey Oswald killed President Kennedy in Dallas everyone was shocked at a life that had been taken too soon. Surely a lone shooter could not bring down the leader of the American establishment within a matter of seconds. The world wanted answers but never got them. After claiming he was just a patsy, Oswald was himself killed before he could give his side of the story.

Back in England Macmillan resigned from being prime minister due to ill health. This should have been the time for Profumo to step up and take the country towards the next decade. But he was gone. Instead, the conservatives chose Lord Alec Douglas-Home, a man who was very much the establishment. Born in 1903, he was certainly never going to be worried that the recently released film *From Russia with Love* had anything to do with him.

As we headed to 1964, *I want to Hold Your Hand* was all over the radio, but the BBC was still trying to control the masses. It lost its grip on broadcasting when Radio Caroline went on air. On television ITV was winning the ratings war. *Ready Steady Go* allowed The Beatles and the Stones to compete on screen. The BBC copied the idea and created *Top of the Pops*. They linked it to the chart singles sales and threatened musicians that if they didn't appear on their show, they wouldn't play their song. The establishment was learning to use modern propaganda to keep power.

But things were beginning to crumble. In 1964 the Conservative Party lost the general election and Labour MP Harold Wilson became prime minister. *The Economist* magazine suggested that the Profumo scandal had helped Labour win and had affected a fundamental and permanent change in relations between politicians and press. Some of the public had also noticed the difference in the way Ward and Profumo had been treated. The idea that the establishment was always right began to be questioned at last. Although a few old dogs found some new tricks.

Long standing Tory Lord Boothby became very close to gangster Ronnie Kray. They had met trying to fund a building project in Enugu, Nigeria. The two mad homosexuals had a mutual admiration for each other's work. One was a member of the House of Lords and had been having an affair with Macmillan's wife for years as well as liking young men. And the other also liked young men as well as being bat shit crazy. When the press mentioned their friendship, Boothby denied he was enjoying the company of Ronnie and rent boys on a regular basis. He sued the papers and won forty thousand pounds, three quarters of a million in today's money. He then handed over all the money to the Krays after they threatened to tell the papers the truth if he didn't. The new Labour government didn't complain too much. The reason being was that Labour MP Tom Driberg was also enjoying the company of young men supplied by Ronnie.

Because politicians were involved, the police were not allowed to investigate the Krays criminal empire for the next couple of years. This meant they continued to have their own special parties and gain power until they started shooting people in pubs. Strangely, just like Stephen Ward it is now believed the Krays were also approached by MI5 to see what they had on the politicians who used their boys and girls and if any of them might be a spy.

Christine came out of prison and did a few more interviews, but by now the Labour government was in power and didn't want to start digging up dirt that might include some old bones of their own. BBC2 started, just in time to watch the first battle between Mods and Rockers on Clacton beach as they talked about their generation. After starting her adventure with the very youthful Ward, Christine had become old before her time.

~

Perhaps that's why people commit suicide. Why try and keep fighting when the game is already rigged against you. Why work only to get taxed nearly half your salary, then taxed on everything you buy, and for what? International companies keep making a profit on former nationalised industries, the rich keep getting richer, and the government seems to spend more money on illegal immigrants and foreign fields than on the pensioners and ancestors who fought for this country.

Modern politicians tell you taxes are going up to try and save the world, yet they can't even fix the potholes in the road. I am reminded of the quote from *Moby Dick,* the story of a man who goes mad chasing a white whale, "There are certain queer times and occasions in this strange mixed affair we call life, when a man takes this whole universe for a vast practical joke, though the wit thereof he but dimly discerns, and more than suspects, that the joke is at nobody's expense but his own." And in the end, it leaves you with the one choice you can still control: the decision to commit suicide.

Chapter 23

Infamy, infamy, they've all got it in for me.

What would have happened if Ward had not died? If he had gone in on that last morning I don't know if it would have changed anything. Both judge and prosecution barrister had been vitriolic throughout the trial and were hardly likely to have a change of heart on the last day. The real issue would be if Ward had been around for sentencing. Anyone convicted of a crime can put in an appeal at the time the sentence is passed. This can be anything from admitting mitigating circumstances, a secret addiction, an elderly aunt that needs looking after, or in Ward's case, the fact that his career as an osteopath was over. It is essentially a call for leniency; to send a man to prison after he has lost everything is a bit like punishing him twice. Unfortunately, as we have already seen, the quality of mercy from this judge was severely strained.

The offence of living off immoral earnings carries a maximum of seven years. Judge Marshall could have combined the two counts, so he served seven years for both at the same time. Her could have also made the two run consecutively, with the next sentence starting straight after the other had finished. That's a possible fourteen years in prison for letting two friends stay in your home and asking them for help to pay the phone bill. Ward's defence barrister would have no doubt appealed the conviction; but it may not have worked.

First, if Ward had been given a prison sentence, every prison governor would be able to move him to a different prison at immediate notice if they received a report that his life was in danger from other prisoners. Ward could have started off in Wormwood Scrubs on Saturday, moved up north to Strangeways in Manchester on Wednesday, then down to Dartmoor by Friday, and on Sunday find himself in Pentonville. Every time Ward would be moved, he would have to re-apply to arrange a legal visit. It could have been months before he would have seen his barrister to make an appeal.

And if he had only gone to prison for a few months, what then? His career as an osteopath would be over. As an artist, he may have wanted a degree of fame and respect, but certainly not one of infamy (he wasn't a writer). All his most famous drawings had been swept up by an anonymous buyer. In another strange occurrence, I am not sure what happened to the money for all his drawings. Did the gallery owner keep it. Did Ward put the cash somewhere safe. What does a fallen man do when he is never able to get himself up?

The police had interviewed numerous people and taken a hundred and forty-seven statements to get Ward into court on spurious charges. They also had another trick up their sleeves. At the time, the police could hold back arresting and charging someone until they were ready. As with Mandy, they may have known about the driving licence and the rented television and could have dealt with both at the same time. They decided not to. Far better to let her know that they could get her again and again and let her think there could be something else coming her way…unless she fully cooperated.

Just before the trial Ward was informed that there were two cases of "helping a woman to procure an abortion" that the police had sitting on file. His crime was that he had passed on a doctor's name to two women wanting a termination. That was it. But it was enough for Ward to face the prospect of another trial. The police could have even been waiting for him at the prison gates on the day he was released.

For the essential fifties gentleman, the sense of an ending was everywhere. For an artist, better to turn the light off with a flick of the switch than slowly fade into obscurity. Within a few years the sharp Mod suits would be replaced by hippy ponchos as the sixties generation tried to tune in and drop out. Ward would have become a caricature from Carry on Camping if he had tried to keep hold of his youth.

~

Looking back, does anyone come out of this with any integrity? For Christine and Mandy, I would argue that they were too young and too scared to understand just how much Ward was being set up. Both had been threatened with prison if they did not comply with the police, and the world for a young single woman was a dangerous place. This was the same year that Fred West married his first wife, and young women were being reported as missing up and down the country. So, you cannot blame them for what happened leading up to and during the trial. Chances are they probably expected Ward to get a slap on the wrist and then sell his story just like they did.

The police involved behaved in a shameful manner. The lying, the deceit, the state sponsored threats to the women involved are surely cause for concern. Every detective involved must have known they were taking part in a corrupt investigation. They were meant to find criminals, not make them. These detectives were not spies bending the rules to see if someone is guilty of being a traitor; they were bringing in young women and threatening them unless they made (up) a statement to charge a man who had committed no crime. How many of them would have done this to their own mother, wife, or daughter? I can accept that the police are a disciplined service; you do as your boss tells you because that's how the chain of command works. They had bills to pay so maybe it was a case of getting the investigation over and hoping that justice would prevail in the end. I can also accept that some of the police officers may have believed they were morally right in bringing Ward to justice. A fifty-year-old man going to orgies and hanging around with women not yet in their twenties probably deserved working on. But as soon as you become the one who decides what is right and wrong, who suffers and who does not, you are essentially no different than Adolf Eichmann sat around a table deciding how to destroy a life purely for political reasons.

And if after a hundred and forty-seven statements the best you had was sweet FA, you should have moved on. As a detective you should have known what was evidential and what was hearsay. And at the point when the same officers sat in the Lucky Gordon trial realised that Christine Keeler had lied on oath and then lied again whilst they sat in the Ward trial, they should have said something. We don't know if any officers were bullied or threatened to stay quiet. The sad thing is those detective constables are not the worse in this sorry saga.

Detective Chief Inspector Herbert was the man running the show. He interviewed Christine more than twenty-five times about Ward, he got Mandy put in prison for having the wrong driving licence then threatened her again unless she helped put Ward away. Herbert died in 1966 whilst investigating the Hammersmith Nudes Murders. After initial praise as a fine upstanding member of the Metropolitan police, it turned out he might have had a few skeletons in the closet. Although nothing was ever made public regarding any corruption complaints, he had somehow managed to hide in his office half a million pounds of cash in today's money. This was at a time when his salary was about a thousand pounds a year.

An internal police enquiry was carried out. Strangely, other police officers could find no evidence of corruption. The cash must have simply fallen into his locked desk drawer. It also transpired that he was sleeping with at least one of the prostitutes who gave evidence against Ward. This means he probably was the only one living off immoral earnings when he stood in the Old Bailey to accuse the defendant. But was he the worst?

The people in MI5 and MI6 were lower than rat's testicles. They knew that Ward had tried to help England in its hour of need. The problem was they had made such a mess of things in relation to Profumo, Ivanov, the Cuban missile crisis, and a host of other faux pars, it would be so much easier if Ward was kept silent, permanently.

There is still a point in British law that anyone convicted of an offence cannot make any money out of the crime, such as writing a book or appearing on television for a fee to talk about the matter. If Ward was convicted a lot of government mistakes would have been buried. If he died, then *all* his secrets would be buried with him.

The politicians who knew Ward had done nothing wrong and yet remained silent were about as morally upright as saggy bags of dog shit hanging from a skinny branch. The Tories wanted the Ward trial to deflect attention away from their poor running of the country. Labour wanted the Ward trial to show the public how poor the Tories were at running the country, and to cover up the mess they were in. Politicians from both sides of the Parliament could have changed the situation but decided not to, possibly for fear of their own indiscretions being exposed. The power of any ruling establishment relies mostly on their perceived power. Getting people to live in fear is a lot easier than what you might expect. Frighten them every so often with stories of war, viruses, famine and fuel bills, and they will willingly hand over their freedoms in the belief you are keeping them safe.

What about the so-called friends who could have saved Ward? Difficult, as no one wants their secrets to be made public. There was a private meeting in a London club where people such as viscount Astor were warned in no uncertain terms that to give evidence in defence of Ward would be tantamount to being made an accomplice. These friends knew that the charges against Ward were merely a sham, but they also knew the establishment had put a lot of time and effort to get it this far. The ruling class were willing to do anything to keep their secrets secret, even if it meant Ward being punished for a crime he had not committed.

As for those involved in the trial itself, the defence barrister Burge could have tried a bit harder to question all the evidence. He could have stated publicly that certain procedures were being abused. No doubt he believed that the appeal for Lucky Gordon would cause this trial to be thrown out. But every trial is directed by the judge. They have the power to refuse evidence, question a witness, and even dismiss a barrister without notice; something which could ruin a career.

It's hard to know if the prosecution barrister Griffith-Jones was doing his job out of duty or some sort of moral calling. Here was a man with the same belief in following orders that we had seen during the Eichmann trial. It didn't matter if people were guilty or innocent, he had been told to get Ward, and that is what he did. He may not have known that Ward would end up killing himself, but he was willing to send him to prison for a couple of years knowing that the charges against him were false. He may have been a ponce, but his only saving grace was that at no point during the trial did the judge try to stop him.

As such, judge Marshall comes out worse than everyone else; and rightly so. He could have refused to sit in judgement, he could have thrown out most of the charges, he could have directed the jury to find Ward not guilty, he could have postponed the trial until Ward recovered, he could have also given a lenient sentence if given the chance; but he did none of these things. Instead, he let a man who was clearly innocent suffer because higher powers wanted to see Ward punished. How many other people had judge Marshall put into prison because of the same reason? But again, he was not acting alone. It really doesn't matter what those with power say their political beliefs are. Left, right, black, white, in the end, those at the top all belong to the same club. And it's a club where maintaining power comes before everything else.

The judges' notes on the trial, and a transcript of his summing up, are considered to be so sensitive that the government has decided they should be kept under The Official Secrets Act and hidden from public view until 2046. At that point the government will carry out another review, and the details could be kept secret even longer. Why? It can only be that the political and justice system at the time of Ward's death all those years ago is still the same systems we have in place now. Details of the investigation into the Bakers Street security vault heist are also being hidden under the Official Secrets Act until the same time.

~

Christine Keeler went on to live a life of relative obscurity. The money from various newspapers quickly disappeared. For a while she had a job as a columnist in a top shelf magazine. But the girl famous for a photograph of her naked behind a chair could not beat the rise of colour mags, videos, DVD's and the internet. What was considered pornographic in the fifties was overtaken by full nude magazines from Europe in the sixties and then swallowed up in the seventies by the rise of X rated films. Unregulated video tapes in the eighties contained stuff that even Ward would have been shocked by. Of course, that was nothing to when the internet arrived at the turn of the millennium. Christine died in in 2017, the year the first robotic sex doll went on sale.

   Mandy Rice-Davies fared a lot better. She described her life as a slow descent into respectability. She made money from her notoriety and kept it. There were a few records and a marriage to a millionaire who ran a few nightclubs in Israel. Her reply when informed in court that Viscount Astor denied having sex with her (well he would, wouldn't he) can still be found today in quotations books. She appeared in a few films, including *Absolute Beginners,* and *Scandal*, based on the Profumo affair. She died in 2014.

   He former lover Peter Rachman also made the dictionary. The idea of the bullying landlord living off the poor became linked to this surname. His henchman Michael De Freitas took over when Rachman died, including the brothels and the crap flat to tenants from the West Indies. He was imprisoned in 1967 after trying to incite people to murder any white man who touched a black woman in the belief that white people were inferior. He moved to the Bahamas and was convicted of murder in 1972 after he attacked a white woman with a machete then buried her whilst she was still alive.

   Lucky Gordon ended up working as a cook at the studios for Island Records, who signed Bob Marley and Amy Winehouse. They probably didn't know the full extent of his crimes. He died in 2017. Johnny Edgecombe seems to be the only person who went to prison for something he had actually done. When released in the sixties he worked as a jazz promoter. He died in 2010.

John Profumo had a pretty good life after politics. He could have helped Ward at his trial by confirming that the doctor had helped the Secret Service for the last few years, but he never. In April 1964 Profumo began working at Toynbee Hall, a charitable organisation based in Spitalfields which supports the most deprived residents in the East End of London. The story is that he spent his time cleaning the place, but this is doubtful. As a president of the charity, he could claim a reasonable salary and expenses, which would be over a hundred thousand pounds a year in today's money. The rich always look after the rich.

He was given the Companion of the Order of the British Empire (CBE) in 1975 and was later described by Prime Minister Margaret Thatcher as a national hero when he was a guest at her 80th birthday celebrations in 2005. The rumour that he took one for the team has never gone away. His marriage to Valerie Hobson lasted until her death in 1998. Profumo died in 2006.

It is now believed that when he was woken up in the middle of the night and taken to Westminster after the scandal broke, he did not tell his colleagues that no sexual impropriety had taken place with Christine Keeler; in fact, he freely admitted it. He wanted to tell the public he had a couple of sexual liaisons with a young woman (he didn't believe it was an affair). He was more worried about being accused of giving away state secrets and wanted to clear his name for that thing only. But he was ordered to lie and say nothing had taken place between him and Christine and hope the true story of the Government and the Secret Service knowing about the situation would fade away. In the end, the establishment was willing to let an individual who could have been a future prime minister be thrown to the wolves for the sake of staying in power. Compared to that, the death of Ward was nothing to them.

The Mews addresses in London are still there, now surrounded by Russian owned flats. Ewhurst Manor in Borehamwood stopped making stag movies in the seventies when the foreign video market took over. The house was knocked and replaced with a small housing estate, often seen in in the background of films such as *George and Mildred*. Cliveden Manor is now a hotel, including the cottage by the river, available for weekend trysts. I like to think that Ward would find the whole thing amusing.

Chapter 24.

They think it's all over. It still isn't now.

So many have gone, and yet so many questions still left unanswered. That's the way with every suicide. You wonder if you could have done more, if you missed something, the silence in reply to a question, if you could have stopped it, the meeting that was never made, could you have done anything different. It's always too late when they've gone. They call it survivors' guilt. You wish you had done more to be a friend when they were alive, but you were always too busy making other plans.

Ward knew shame when his private life was turned into a series of public accusations. He knew sadness when his friends deserted him at his lowest point. Ward didn't die because he was guilty, he sacrificed himself because he knew he was innocent.

It seems strange that so much has been written about the death of President Kennedy on the basis that it was part of a conspiracy theory; and yet a real conspiracy to permanently silence an Englishman in the same year seems to go unnoticed. If Ward had been a traitor, he would have been charged with that. You could also argue that if the government was really believed Stephen Ward had secrets they did not want the public to know, why not kill him before any trial? The answer is in the difference between government and establishment. The establishment has the power, the government maintains it. The establishment doesn't want to get its hands dirty, the government decides the rules, decides the laws, decides life and death. Ward knew establishment secrets, not government ones. No point shooting him, it would make too many people scared that this was a lone gunman, a jealous husband, an argument over the rent. The trial was public, he could be shown to have broken the law; what happened to him afterwards would be in private. Governments don't like to have their secrets exposed.

In July 1963 America was gearing up for the presidential election race. They had been aware of Ward for the last few years and certainly would have wanted to know if there was anything that might come back to bite Kennedy. Thanks to his links with Mariella Novotny, they must have believed there was. His death was a very succinct way of making sure those secrets remained safe. In 1984 Mariella told people she was going to write her life story. A few weeks later she was found dead of a suspected drug overdose.

~

When I think about Stephen standing in the dock, I am reminded of the falling man from the Twin Towers; someone caught up in circumstances beyond their control and makes the ultimate final decision. When the hijacked plane hit the building, I am sure the man believed they would escape or be rescued. But as events became more serious, he knew that would not be the case. He smashed a window on the hundredth floor, climbed out, positioned himself to look down on the world below, and then jumped. It would have taken about ten seconds before he hit the ground. If you count to ten in your head, that's how long he was falling. Perhaps he thought a moment of pain before death was better than a lifetime of suffering. Is this the real answer to why people commit suicide? *The situation I am in so meaningless, and I am so trapped, that leaving my life is better than living it.* Somehow a series of events that may have started years ago that may mean nothing at the time (when the hijackers took flying lessons in America, they didn't bother attending the lessons on how to land a plane) can gain a momentum of their own until things begin to spiral out of control. From a series of circumstances, the Falling Man found himself standing one the ledge a hundred floors up on the morning of 9/11.

And still the question, why would Stephen Ward want to kill himself? Is the answer in his choice of death. The son of a vicar did not hang from a rope like Judas. Perhaps the idea was too close to how others perceived the faker that Ward had now been painted as by reporters. To lie in the bath and cut his wrists would be somehow sinful for a medical man. As part of the Medical Corps in thew war, a gun might portray him as his own worst enemy. Death by machine, a car, or a train, seems far too ugly. After sitting through the Eichmann trial and seeing how millions of Jews were killed, an oven or gas fire would make his own death seem insignificant.

Instead, Ward chose the Socratic way out. Don't let the government have full control over your life by choosing the moment when you are going to die. As he stood in the dock listening to the first part of the summing up, he knew that no matter what happened in a court of law, in the public's eye's he was already portrayed as guilty. No matter what decision the jury came to, he knew he was already falling and decided to do something before he hit rock bottom.

I don't know how long he had carried a blank prescription book in his pocket for. He could have been waiting months, ever since the press and police started watching him. It could have been put there after three weeks of being remanded in prison. There was a moment a week before the trial when he had a major exhibition of his portraits in a Chelsea gallery. Ward saw Mandy at the exhibition, a glass of wine in her hand. He went over to ask the young woman who had tried to kill herself less than a year before how she was doing. She told him she had to go meet her connection in the press and walked away. Maybe that was when he knew it was over. He those he always thought were slightly beneath him were walking away. What we can say is that he had that prescription pad with him on the day judge Marshall began his summing up and told Ward that Christine lying on oath was to be taken as the truth. And in a place where every word carries with it the power to change lives, he knew it was over. How can a man be the hero of his own story when fact and fiction no longer have any meaning?

Does it matter if Ward simply asked to stop the car outside Harrods and got his friend to run into the chemist to get some tablets because he could not sleep? Surely this was just like so many people today taking something to help get them through the night. The meal with friends that evening appeared to show a man ready for tomorrow, and even the day after that. He wrote some letters, but these were if he was convicted and sent to prison without getting a chance to speak to the press. His girlfriend, the last known person to see him alive, said that he did not seem concerned. Perhaps Ward was able to hide his true feelings until he was alone.

Perhaps there was a moment in the darkness when he had a blinding vision and realised nothing made sense anymore. Life had become meaningless. Money, reputation, relationships, art, health, did not matter in those final minutes. He simply swallowed one tablet, then another, then another, and kept up that petty pace until the words stopped.

~

Has anything really changed in the last sixty years? Many men still spend most of their lives hanging on in quiet desperation. You watch a government that seems totally incompetent somehow blame you for all the problems of the world. It all feels like the universe is playing a vast practical joke being played on you.

Today we may know more about what causes men to commit suicide, but that doesn't mean we are doing anything about it. With something such as depression we are aware that it is more common than many people realise. It can last a short time, a few months, even years, and in the end it does eventually lift. It can also come back, sometimes through internal factors such as health, sometimes from external factors. There are various types of medication on the market, and therapy. It's been found that talking helps; maybe that's why women hold back from taking their own lives more than men.

We also know people get depressed through a physical ailment such as a bad back. Chronic pain can lead to a lack of sleep. Add to that the long-term use of painkillers, age and drink, and it becomes a mental battle. For others it is a chemical change in the brain that can trip you up. We still do not know how much years of processed food and computer games is affecting our way of thinking. Add to that the virtual world. Social media has allowed the meek to inherit the earth, and it turns out they are more vicious and vindictive with their words than the bullies who pushed you in the playground. External circumstances also affect men far more than what they say. Changes in their financial situation, a breakdown in relationships, issues at work, getting old, all take their toll. If Stephen Ward was in the same situation today, would he still take his life?

Chapter 25.

You can't always get what you want.

There are some songs that give you a sense of sad nostalgia. Is it the music or the memory that does it. The song may be melancholy, or it may be linked to the regret of the words we never said, the actions we never took. The weird thing is, we may listen to that song over and over again. Perhaps it's a classic, a work of art, or sometimes it's to get away from the sheer ordinariness of life. Something to drown out the day-to-day noise of mediocrity. Sometimes the sad songs never seem to stop.

The Profumo scandal signalled the fifties was over and the sixties had truly begun. No more debutantes in ball gowns. Young girls were now screaming to the Beatles and the Stones. No more getting up at dawn to do your National Service. Instead, men put on Italian suits and danced all night. Teenagers didn't want to listen to the BBC on the radio anymore. And the press, once the only form of news, was being overshadowed by television. 1963 was the end of black and white history and the start of a bright shiny future. But sometimes it's easier to hide things in the light than in the darkness.

Since Ward's death there have been films and TV shows about the Profumo scandal, often with Ward played as a side character in his own trial. The film *Scandal* was released in 1989. It is an interesting account of what happened, especially when the producers openly said that a lot of people in power warned them against telling the whole story.

In 2013 Andrew Lloyd Webber produced a musical based on Ward's last few years. It was OK, but the audience wanted another *Cabaret* or *Chicago*, rather than a miscarriage of justice where the hero kills himself at the end. They wanted more soap in their opera. In 2019 the BBC produced *The trial of Christine Keeler*. This is probably the poorest version of events, as it cannot help but delve into the modern social politics of feminism and racism rather than dealing with the true story.

There have been books about Ward and the Profumo scandal. Christine wrote her account of events a couple of times over the years. Some have tried to get to the truth; but all face the same problem of not being able to see the files about the investigation. Even the court transcript (which is usually made public if the defendant is found guilty) is classified as top secret and not allowed to be seen by the public for many years yet to come.

It's almost as if no one wants to look too closely at the trial because we will realise it was a travesty of justice committed by our own government. Although Lord Denning always asserted that Ward's trial and conviction was fair and proper, most modern commentators believe it was deeply flawed. One judge said that he would have stopped the trial before it reached court. It's the same when people pass away. We can all agree that we would have done something…if we had known at the time…if someone had just said something. But it's always too late when they've gone.

The human rights lawyer Geoffrey Robertson has campaigned since the 1990's for the Ward case to be reopened on several grounds: the premature scheduling of the trial, the lack of evidence to support the main charges, the numerous misdirection's by the judge in his summing up, and above all, judge Marshall failure to properly advise the jury that Christine Keeler had committed perjury in the Gordon trial. All of which is true. Which leads to the question: Why has Ward not been given a pardon yet?

The mathematician Alan Turing was convicted in 1952 of Gross Indecency after admitting to being in a consensual sexual relationship with a nineteen-year-old man when homosexuality was still illegal. His work at Bletchley was so secretive that it couldn't even be told to the court during his trial. He was sentenced to have a form of chemical castration where his testosterone was reduced to the point where he started to grow breasts. One night as if enacting a scene from *Snow White* he poured poison onto an apple and ate it. His cleaner found him in bed the next day. The verdict was suicide. After a series of high-profile celebrities pointed out the unfairness of it all he was given a posthumous pardon in 2013. Soon after the government decided that everyone convicted of a homosexual offence before 1967 would be given a pardon. Perhaps we should expand that generosity to all those wrongly convicted of any offence especially those who killed themselves because of it.

Stephen Ward's work on behalf of MI5 was finally confirmed in 1982 when *The Sunday Times* located his former contact named "Woods". Now an old man, he admitted that the Government had used Ward for their own gain and had lied when the Profumo scandal was exposed. The government were aware they could have saved him, but it would have meant some officials would have been embarrassed by their failure to not carry out their duties accordingly. At least Woods got to grow old. Although it seems every successive government continues to make the same mistakes.

The war in Iraq, lasting from 2003 to 20012, was based on a bright shining lie. America wanted revenge for 9/11. British prime minister Tony Blair wanted the public to believe Saddam Hussein had weapons of mass destruction. Rumours appeared in the media that missile bases had been built on the border and that the warheads could contain nuclear and biological weapons. Dr David Kelly, and expert in biological warfare, knew the information was false. He spoke to a BBC journalist, who released the conversation without it being sanctioned. The labour government witchfinder general Alistair Campbell demanded to know where the information had come from. The BBC journalist threw Kelly under the bus and named him. The government decided to make an example of Kelly to stop others talking.

An inquiry was set up which had the power to summon people to give evidence. Kelly was interrogated by the *Parliamentary Intelligence and Security and Foreign Affairs Select committee*. It was a show trial. Most people agree that the questioning by labour politicians was extremely hostile towards Kelly, who wanted him to take the blame and distract attention away from the government starting an illegal war. Although he declined to answer many questions during the committee hearing, afterwards, Dr Kelly said he would go public with what he really knew about the government cover up. The government knew that every press agency was restricted in how much they could report. In times of war the normal rules do not apply, even if you started it.

Two days later Dr Kelly was found dead. He had apparently gone for a walk into some nearby woods, where he took some pills, and managed to cut his wrists as well. The coroner quickly listed it as suicide, but many felt that foul play was involved. The drugs should not have killed him so quickly, and way the wrists had been cut could not have been done by Dr Kelly. The report into the death of Dr Kelly is now kept locked under the Official Secrets Act. Strange how after all this time, the deaths of Dr Ward in 1963, and Dr Kelly in 2003, are being hidden away by the government under the guise of keeping the country safe.

We always want to believe we would be on the right side of history. We would not be like Adolf Eichmann and blindly carrying out orders. We would be the Romans who let the Christians pray, the plantation slave owners who would treat the blacks as equals, the Germans who hid Jews in the basement. If we thought the establishment was morally wrong, we would do something about it. What is more, if Stephen Ward was our friend, even though we might be shocked at his personal life, we would have testified that he was innocent of the charges brought against him, wouldn't we?

In January 2014 Ward's trial was considered by the Criminal Cases Review Commission, which has the power to investigate suspected miscarriages of justice and refer unlawful convictions to the Court of Appeal. It decided the original decision was to stand. We are still not allowed to see the full details of his trial. Perhaps the question shouldn't be how did the establishment get away with the death of an innocent man, but how did we let it happen? The answer is simple, we were distracted. After a diet of false information and dubious distractions, we missed the chance to do something about those in power. We are still being distracted today.

In the end I believe that Ward wanted to take his own life. Whether there were others involved who gave him a helping hand it doesn't really matter. Not letting a corrupt judge decide his fate in a trial filled with lies was the last honest decision of a man who knew he could never beat the system alone.

~

If you really want to kill yourself then the only thing I can say is…wait. Wait until tomorrow, wait a week, a month, or set a date for exactly one year's time. Let each day creep at its own petty pace while you try to find meaning and get your life in order. Go outside and walk every day and give yourself a goal of adding more steps every month. Be grateful when you go out and the sun is shining on your face rather than your grave. Go get a dog from a local rescue centre, look after it for exactly a year by giving it all the love and attention it deserves; then on the day you decide to kill yourself, kill the dog first. Don't think you can do it. Think that its cruel. Then think about the people who are going to deal with their emotions after you've gone. And while we are here, tell people how you feel. Chances are many will be fighting battles you can't see.

My other advice is to read more. Not the crap I write, this isn't *Catcher in the Rye*. What I mean is read a book that interests you. Leonardo Da Vinci, Albert Einstein, Winston Churchill, none of them had access to the number of books you have today. Whether it's history or fiction (sometimes both), spend time every day reading a chapter until you find yourself reading two chapters and then the whole book.

The next thing is to meet old friends. It doesn't have to be in the pub, make it the local café. Join a group that are involved in a hobby you want to do. Everyone has to start somewhere. And if you believe life is meaningless, why are you so worried about what other people are going to think of you? Finally, remember the Latin phrase *Illegitimi non carborundum*, which roughly translates as *Don't let the Bastards grind you down.*

Footnote. In 2022 the former prime minister Tony Blair was acquitted of any misdoing in relation to starting an illegal war in the middle east and was given a knighthood.

Printed in Great Britain
by Amazon